HOT RODS

A Problem-Based Unit

The College of William and Mary
School of Education
Center for Gifted Education
Williamsburg, Virginia 23185

HOT RODS

A Problem-Based Unit

The College of William and Mary
School of Education
Center for Gifted Education
Williamsburg, Virginia 23185

Center for Gifted Education Staff:
Project Director: Dr. Joyce VanTassel-Baska
Project Managers: Dr. Shelagh A. Gallagher
Dr. Victoria B. Damiani
Project Consultants: Dr. Beverly T. Sher
Linda Neal Boyce
Dana T. Johnson
Dennis R. Hall
Donna L. Poland

Teacher Developer:
Rebecca F. Crossett

funded by Jacob K. Javits,
United States Department of Education

KENDALL/HUNT PUBLISHING COMPANY
4050 Westmark Drive   Dubuque, Iowa 52002

Copyright © 1997 by Center for Gifted Education

ISBN 0-7872-2813-3

Printed in the United States of America

10   9   8   7   6   5   4   3   2   1

CONTENTS

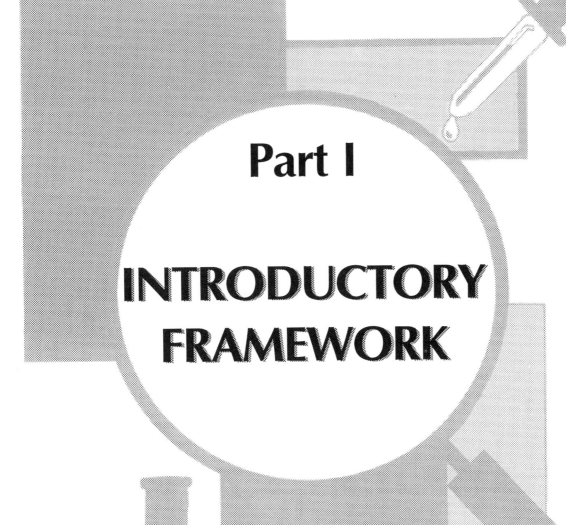

Part I

INTRODUCTORY FRAMEWORK

INTRODUCTION

Hot Rods is a problem-based science unit designed for high ability learners. Elements of the unit have been successfully used with all learners in a wide variety of situations, from pull-out programs for gifted learners to traditional heterogeneously grouped classrooms. It allows middle school students to explore a variety of "systems" in a novel way, namely through the process of grappling with an ill-structured, "real-world" problem.

Because the unit is problem-based, the way in which a teacher implements the unit will necessarily differ from the way in which most traditional science units are used. Preparing for and implementing problem-based learning takes time, flexibility, and a willingness to experiment with a new way of teaching.

The total time required for completion of *Hot Rods* should be minimally 30 hours, with more time required for additional activities.

RATIONALE AND PURPOSE

This unit has been designed to introduce the overarching science concept of systems to high-ability middle school students through the use of the teaching technique of problem-based learning. A variety of systems, including nuclear power plant systems and social systems are presented in the context of a simulated real-world problem. The need to come up with a resolution for this unit problem engages student interest and provides all of the direction for the intellectual movement within the unit. Through the problem-based process, students will acquire significant science content knowledge in areas such as nuclear physics and biology; they will also model the scientific process in their search for information necessary for the resolution of the problem. This information will be obtained not only from books and other traditional resource materials but also from hands-on experimentation and from outside resource people, including practicing scientists.

GOALS AND OUTCOMES

➥ To understand the concept of systems

Students will be able to apply the ideas involved in the systems concept to the analysis of a variety of systems, including biological systems, nuclear power systems, and social systems.

SYSTEMS OUTCOMES

A. For each system, students will be able to use appropriate systems language to identify boundaries, important elements, input, and output.

B. Students will be able to analyze the interactions of various system components with each other and with input into the system, both for the real-world systems and for the experimental systems.

C. Based on their understanding of each system's functioning, students will be able to predict the impact of various kinds of inputs on the system.

D. Students will be able to transfer their knowledge about systems in general to a newly encountered system. In the final assessment activity, students will be given a new system to analyze in the same way that they have analyzed the systems in the unit.

E. Students will analyze several systems during the course of the unit. These include nuclear reactions as systems, nuclear power plants and the political and social system that surrounds the issue of nuclear power.

➥ To design scientific experiments necessary to solve given problems

In order to solve these scientific problems, students will be able to design, perform, and report on the results of a number of experiments.

SCIENTIFIC PROCESS OUTCOMES

A. Students will be able to explore a new scientific area, including nuclear physics in the realm of nuclear power production.

B. Students will be able to identify meaningful scientific problems for investigation during the course of working through the central unit problem and its ramifications.

C. During their experimental work, students will:

—Demonstrate good data-handling skills

—Analyze any experimental data as appropriate

—Evaluate their results in light of the original problem

—Use their enhanced understanding of the area under study to make predictions about similar problems whose answers are not yet known to the student

—Communicate their enhanced understanding of the scientific area to others

➥ To understand the principles associated with various aspects of nuclear power

SPECIFIC CONTENT OUTCOMES

A. Students will be able to describe the process of nuclear fission and explain how this process generates energy.

B. Students will be able to explain the difference between a radioactive isotope and a stable isotope of the same element.

C. Students will be able to describe the physical properties and biological effects of several different kinds of decay products that result from radioactive decay, including alpha particles, beta particles, neutrons, and gamma rays (electromagnetic radiation).

D. Students will be able to explain the concept of half-life and use this concept to predict how much of a radioactive substance with a known half-life will remain after a set time.

E. Students will be able to explain how a chain reaction works and to model one, both physically and conceptually.

F. Students will be able to explain (in general terms) how a fission reactor produces energy and how its energy production rate is controlled.

G. Students will be able to describe the uses of shielding materials, both for nuclear power plants and for other applications.

H. Students will experimentally investigate the shielding properties of various materials for a safe form of electromagnetic radiation, either visible or ultraviolet light.

I. Students will be able to describe the problem of storage of nuclear waste and to discuss the relative merits and deficiencies of various solutions to this problem.

J. Students will be able to evaluate the relative risks of nuclear power and of other power-generation methods, both to nearby consumers and to future generations.

ASSESSMENT

This unit contains many assessment opportunities that can be used to monitor student progress and assess student learning. Opportunities for formative assessment include:

- The student's problem log, a written compilation of the student's thoughts about the problem. Each lesson contains suggested questions for students to answer in their problem logs. The problem log should also be used by the student to record data and new information that they have obtained during the course of the unit.

- Experimental design worksheets, which can be used to assess a student's understanding of experimental design and the scientific process, as well as to record information about what was done and what was found during student-directed experimentation.

- Other forms throughout the unit which are used to help the student explain their solutions to particular parts of the problem.
- Teacher observation of student participation in large-group and small-group activities.
- Final unit assessments allow the teacher to determine whether individual students have met the science process, science content, and systems objectives listed in the Goals and Objectives section at the beginning of the unit.

SAFETY PRECAUTIONS TO BE TAKEN IN THE LAB

As this unit involves laboratory work, some general safety procedures should be observed at all times. Some districts will have prescribed laboratory safety rules; for those that do not, some basic rules to follow for this unit and any other curriculum involving scientific experimentation are:

1. Students must behave appropriately in the lab. No running or horseplay should be allowed; materials should be used for only the intended purposes.
2. No eating, drinking, or smoking in lab; no tasting of laboratory materials. No pipetting by mouth.
3. If students are using heat sources, such as alcohol burners, long hair must be tied back and loose clothing should be covered by a lab coat.
4. Fire extinguishers should be available; students should know where they are and how to use them.
5. Caution: Dry ice must be handled with care. Please note the dry ice safety instructions in Lesson 7.
6. Radioactive materials can be hazardous. Please follow all safety guidelines provided by the supplier of the radioactive materials.
7. If a commercial research-type UV source is being used, it will be necessary for students to wear plastic UV-protective glasses; long-term exposure to UV can cause cataracts. Also, direct illumination of the skin by the UV source should be avoided; it is possible to be sunburned by these sources.

MATERIALS LIST

Materials needed for each individual lesson are listed in the "Materials and Handouts" section of the lesson.

LESSON FLOW CHART

Problem-based learning is not easy to plan, because it is driven by student questioning and interest. We have included estimated durations for each lesson in this unit, but be prepared to be flexible and to move with the students. We have also included a diagram (Figure 1) which shows the relationship between the individual lessons and experiments suggested in the unit. In general, lessons shown higher in the diagram are prerequisites for those shown lower in the diagram. Be aware that this diagram may not reflect all of the time that you will need to spend; students may well come up with unanticipated, yet valid, experiments or lines of questioning.

We feel that some of the lessons are essential for all students, while others can be done with a subgroup as long as the subgroup reports its results back to the whole class.

TAILORING *HOT RODS* TO YOUR LOCATION

Some general considerations in localizing the *Hot Rods* problem include:

1. Involve local experts (power company representative, nuclear researcher, Nuclear Regulatory Commission representative, physicist, etc.) as speakers and on-going resources in the problem-solving process.

2. Work with librarians to plan the unit and to assist students in finding information. In addition to school librarians and academic librarians, special libraries (museums, corporations, historical societies, etc.) offer vast resources relevant to the unit.

3. If your school is near a nuclear power plant, you may want to change some of the details or data in this unit to match those of your community. You should include a trip to the power plant. In addition to the experts mentioned above, you may have a citizen's group that monitors issues dealing with the power plant visit the class-room. Since a number of lessons encourage students to look at various points of view, a group such as this might be a valuable resource.

GLOSSARY OF TERMS

Alpha Particle: The positively charged particle emitted in the radioactive decay of certain radioactive atoms. An alpha particle is identical to the nucleus of the helium atom.

Atom: The smallest part of a chemical element that has all the chemical properties of that element.

Atomic Number: The number of protons in the nucleus of an atom. There is a separate atomic number for each element. The atomic number is used to identify atoms as gold, oxygen, or some other element.

FIGURE 1

LESSON FLOW CHART

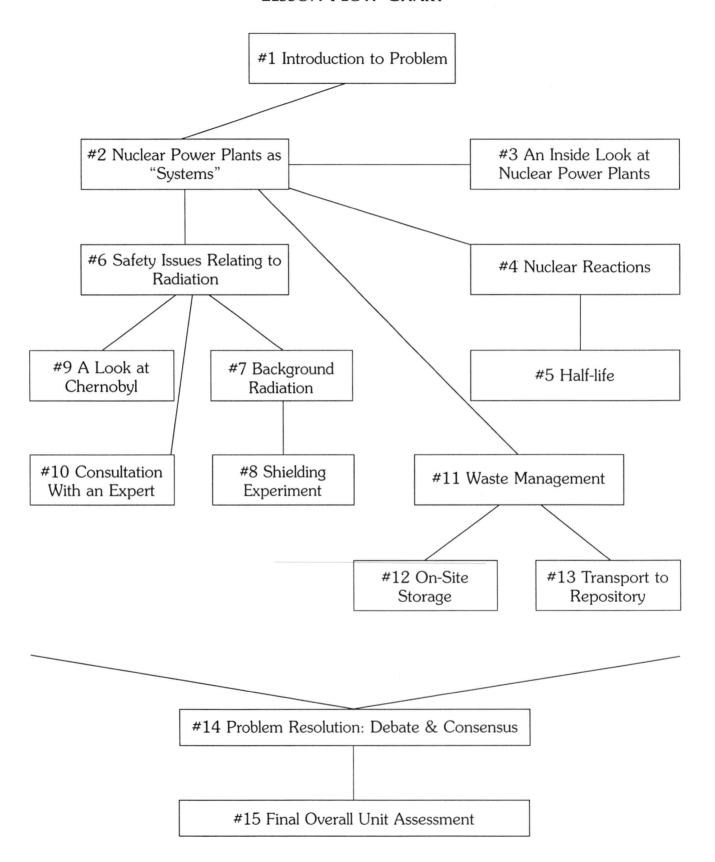

#1 Introduction to Problem

#2 Nuclear Power Plants as "Systems"

#3 An Inside Look at Nuclear Power Plants

#6 Safety Issues Relating to Radiation

#4 Nuclear Reactions

#9 A Look at Chernobyl

#7 Background Radiation

#5 Half-life

#10 Consultation With an Expert

#8 Shielding Experiment

#11 Waste Management

#12 On-Site Storage

#13 Transport to Repository

#14 Problem Resolution: Debate & Consensus

#15 Final Overall Unit Assessment

Atomic Weight: The sum of the protons and neutrons in the nucleus of an atom.

Background Radiation: The natural radioactivity in the environment. Background radiation consists of cosmic radiation from outer space, radiation from the radioactive elements in rocks and soil, and radiation from radon and its decay products in the air we breathe.

Beta Particle: A negatively charged particle that is emitted by certain radioactive atoms. A beta particle is identical to the electron.

Boundary (Systems): Something that indicates or fixes a limit on the extent of the system.

Decay Product: The isotope produced by the decay of a radioactive isotope.

Electromagnetic Spectrum: The complete range of frequencies of electromagnetic waves from the lowest to the highest, including radio infrared, visible light, ultraviolet x-ray, gamma ray, and cosmic ray waves.

Electron: A subatomic particle with a negative charge. The electron circles the nucleus of an atom.

Element (Systems): A distinct part of the system; a component of a complex entity (system).

Fission: The splitting of a fissionable nucleus into two smaller, nearly equal, radioactive nuclei, accompanied by the emission of two or more neutrons and a significant amount of energy. Fission in a nuclear reactor is initiated by the fissionable nucleus absorbing a neutron.

Fuel Assembly: A grouping of nuclear fuel rods that is put into or taken out of a nuclear reactor core as a unit. The reactor core is made up of a collection of fuel assemblies.

Gamma Ray: Gamma radiation emitted during the radioactive decay of certain radioactive materials.

Half-life: The amount of time needed for half of the atoms in a quantity of a radioisotope to decay.

Input (Systems): Something that is put in the system; an addition to the components of the system.

Isotope: Atoms of the same element that have equal numbers of protons but differing numbers of neutrons.

Monitored Retrievable Storage (MRS) Facility: A temporary surface storage system being studied by the U.S. Department of Energy as part of an integrated system for disposing of spent nuclear fuel.

Neutron: A subatomic particle that appears in the nucleus of all atoms except hydrogen. Neutrons have no electrical charge.

Nuclear Chain Reaction: In a nuclear chain reaction, a fissionable nucleus absorbs a neutron and splits into two smaller, nearly equal nuclei, releasing additional neutrons. These in turn can be absorbed by other fissionable nuclei, releasing still more neutrons. This give rise to a self-sustaining reaction.

Nuclear Radiation: Ionizing radiation (alpha, beta, and gamma) originating in the nuclei of radioactive atoms.

Nuclear Waste: Radioactive by-products from any activity including energy and weapons production, as well as, medical treatment and research.

Nucleus: The central part of an atom that contains the protons and neutrons.

Output (Systems): Something that is produced by the system; a product of the system interactions.

Proton: A subatomic particle in the nucleus of an atom with about the same mass as the neutron but carrying a positive charge.

Radiation: Energy that moves through space in the form of particles or electromagnetic waves.

Radioactive Decay: The spontaneous giving off of an alpha or beta particle or a gamma ray by a radioisotope.

Radioactivity: The property possessed by some elements, such as uranium, of spontaneously emitting alpha or beta particles or gamma rays.

Radioisotope: A naturally occurring or artificially created radioactive isotope of a chemical element.

Scientific Process (or Research): The scientific research process can be described by the following steps:

1. Learn a great deal about your field.
2. Think of a good (interesting, important, and tractable) problem.
3. Decide which experiments/observations/calculations would contribute to a solution of the problem.
4. Perform the experiments/observations/calculations.
5. Decide whether the results really do contribute to a better understanding of the problem. If they do not, return to either step 2 (if you're very discouraged) or step 3. If they do, go to step 6.
6. Communicate your results to as many people as possible. If they're patentable, tell a lawyer before you tell anyone else, and write a patent application or two. Publish them in a scientific journal (or if they are really neat, in *The New York Times*); go to conferences and talk about them; tell all of your friends.

Spent Fuel: Fuel that has been used in a nuclear reactor and then withdrawn. Spent fuel is thermally hot and highly radioactive.

System: A group of interacting, interrelated, or interdependent elements forming a complex whole.

Transuranic: Having an atomic number greater than 92; elements with atomic numbers higher than the atomic number for uranium (92).

Ultraviolet Light: Light with wavelength shorter than visible light, but longer than x-rays.

LETTER TO PARENTS

Dear Parent or Guardian:

Your child is about to begin a science unit that uses an instructional strategy called problem-based learning. In this unit students will take a very active role in identifying and resolving a "real-world" problem constructed to promote science learning. Your child will not be working out of a textbook during this unit but will be gathering information from a variety of other sources both in and out of school.

The goals for the unit are:

- *To understand the concept of "systems."*

    Students will be able to analyze several systems during the course of the unit. These include the biological systems, nuclear power systems, and social systems. In addition, all experiments set up during the course will be treated as systems.

- *To understand the principles associated with various aspects of nuclear power.*

    —Students will be able to describe the process of nuclear fission and explain how this process generates energy.

    —Students will be able to explain the difference between a radioactive isotope and a stable isotope of the same element.

    —Students will be able to describe the physical properties and biological effects of several different kinds of decay products that result from radioactive decay, including alpha particles, beta particles, neutrons, and gamma rays (electromagnetic radiation).

    —Students will be able to explain the concept of half-life and use this concept to predict how much of a radioactive substance with a known half-life will remain after a set time.

    —Students will be able to explain how a chain reaction works and to model one, both physically and conceptually.

    —Students will be able to explain (in general terms) how a fission reactor produces energy and how its energy production rate is controlled.

    —Students will be able to describe the uses of shielding materials, both for nuclear power plants and for other applications.

    —Students will experimentally investigate the shielding properties of various materials for a safe form of electromagnetic radiation, either visible or ultraviolet light.

    —Students will be able to describe the problem of storage of nuclear waste and to discuss the relative merits and deficiencies of various solutions to this problem.

—Students will be able to evaluate the relative risks of nuclear power and of other power-generation methods, both to nearby consumers and to future generations.

- *To design scientific experiments necessary to solve given problems.*

  In order to solve scientific problems, students need to be able to design, perform, and report on the results of a number of experiments. During their experimental work, students will:

  —Demonstrate good data-handling skills

  —Analyze any experimental data as appropriate

  —Evaluate their results in the light of the original problem

  —Use their enhanced understanding of the area under study to make predictions about similar problems whose answers are not yet known to the student

  —Communicate their enhanced understanding of the scientific area to others

Since we know from educational research that parental involvement is a strong factor in promoting positive attitudes toward science, we encourage you to extend your child's school learning through activities in the home.

Ways that you may wish to help your child during the learning of this unit include:

- Discuss systems, including family systems, educational systems, etc.

- Discuss the problem they have been given.

- Engage your child in scientific-experimentation exercises based on everyday events such as: In a grocery store, how would you test whether it's better to go in a long line with people having few items or a short line with people having full carts?

- Take your child to area science museums and the library to explore how scientists solve problems.

- Use the problem-based learning model to question students about a question they have about the real world, e.g., How does hail form? Answer: What do you know about hail? What do you need to know to answer the question? How do you find out?

Thank you in advance for your interest in your child's curriculum. Please do not hesitate to contact me for further information as the unit progresses.

Sincerely,

Part II

LESSON PLANS

Introduction to the Problem

LESSON LENGTH: 3-5 sessions

INSTRUCTIONAL PURPOSE

- To introduce students to the problem.
- To help students organize information.
- To create a visual chart of topics that need to be considered in order to understand a balanced perspective of nuclear energy systems.

MATERIALS AND HANDOUTS

Supplementary information: maps, medical reports, newspaper articles to be provided as issues are raised by students (see Supplementary Information at the end of Lesson 1)

Chart paper

Handout 1.1: Problem Statement
Handout 1.2: "Need to Know" board
Handout 1.3: Problem Log Questions
Handout 1.4: Problem Log Questions
Handout 1.5: Problem Log Questions

Session 1

THINGS TO DO

1. Pass out the copies of the Problem Statement (Handout 1.1) and have students read it.

2. Organize the problem statement into three categories on the "Need to Know" board (Handout 1.2). Prioritize the "Need to Know" board from "most to least critical."

3. As students generate questions for the "Need to Know" board, ask them to tell why the information is important or what idea they are

pursuing by asking for the information. These will act as initial "hypothesis" statements.

4. Debate reasons for prioritizing choices. Ask students to identify resources that will help them answer or further investigate the elements of the "Need to Know" board. Divide the learning issues among students so that each student (or a different group of students) will bring different information to the class on the following session.

5. Have students complete Problem Log Questions (Handout 1.3).

THINGS TO ASK

- What's going on?

- What are we supposed to do?

- What kinds of questions do you think the press will ask you?

- What are the questions you have in your mind?

- What additional information would you like to have about the power plant? About CAFSE's side of the issue?

- Where can we find the answers to these questions?

- Do you have any ideas right now about what to do?

- What seems to be the main problem?

- Are there other problems? What could they be?

- What's the best way to proceed to get this information?

Session 2

NOTE TO TEACHER

Prior to these sessions, assemble the supplementary information pages (at the end of this lesson) into packets for various groups.

THINGS TO DO

1. Provide the additional information about the expansion issue (best if provided as "primary sources"—medical reports, letters, diagrams, maps, etc.). You may distribute the packets that contain the supplementary information found at the end of this lesson. Allow for some time for in-class research if necessary, or assign a "task force" to go to the library.

2. Have students report on the information they found overnight. Ask them to look over the "Need to Know" board and identify: 1) what questions they have answered; and 2) what new questions arise out of their new information. Next, ask students what they are going to need to know in order to solve the problem. Prioritize the list based on negotiations with students.

3. Encourage students to refine their speculations about the nature of the problem, the size of the problem and the pervasiveness of the problem (is this just a problem for Riverton or is it a problem for other people in the state? the country?)

THINGS TO ASK

- What questions are answered by the new information?
- What questions do we still have to answer?
- What new questions do you have?
- What are the things we may have to learn about to address the problem?
- Is the problem different today than it was yesterday?
- How are we going to solve this problem?
- What sort of strategies should we use?

ASSESSMENT

Answer questions in Handout 1.4.

NOTE TO TEACHER

The supplementary information presented in this lesson was generated as a result of questions asked by the pilot test classes as they tried to unravel the problem. It is possible that other students will raise questions which are not answered by these documents. Teachers may have to supplement this information with their own original documents.

Session 3

THINGS TO DO

1. Discuss the upcoming Town Meeting and how to best present a full picture of nuclear energy to the public.

2. Place the words "Nuclear Energy" in the center of a large piece of chart paper, circle the words, and have students think about what knowledge people have to have in order to understand nuclear energy. Students can create the web by clustering the information the public needs to know about nuclear energy around the central circle.

3. Students should refer to the public notice from the mayor and pick out specific phrases that would be important for the public to understand. It would be important to make sure this information is included on the web.

4. Questioning should become more precise as students create the web of information that will have to be addressed at the town meeting. For example, if it is important to learn about a nuclear power plant, students should cluster specific questions about a nuclear power plant around that segment of the web. (How does a nuclear power plant work? How is a power plant constructed? What is the difference between a nuclear power plant and an electrical power plant?) However, to keep students from straying too far afield in their web, it is important that they always consider the context of the problem. Not all issues related to nuclear power may be important to this specific problem!

5. Through tutorial questioning and reference to the "Need to Know" board, students can spend a full session developing a web of the knowledge base of nuclear energy.

6. The web can be used and referred to throughout the unit. As topics are covered, they can be shaded in. As questions arise on the "Need to Know" board, they can be integrated into the web related to other aspects of the nuclear knowledge base.

7. Segments of the web can be assigned to individuals or groups of students to investigate. Give out Handout 1.5 to help students focus on their areas of interest.

THINGS TO ASK

- What information does the public need to understand about nuclear energy in order to make an informed decision at the town meeting?

- What scientific knowledge will we have to present at the meeting in order for the public to understand nuclear energy?

- What group or groups do you think will be attending the Town Meeting?

- What do you think their primary concerns will be?

- What kinds of questions do you think these people will want to have answered?

- In order to understand the main nuclear energy questions, what specific questions do we need to have answered?

- Are we outlining information that is unbiased?

- Will understanding this information help the public to see both the positive and negative issues of nuclear power?

ASSESSMENT

1. Quality of web, including appropriate connections between topics.
2. Quality of questions raised.
3. Comprehensiveness of perspective.

NOTE TO TEACHER

Look ahead to Lesson 6 and order the document *Aging Nuclear Power Plants* using the order form at the end of the lesson.

HANDOUT 1.1

PROBLEM STATEMENT

Your name is Christine Barrett, and you are the mayor of the town of Riverton. You have a nice home on the Back River with your husband Richard, a middle school teacher for the Riverton School District, and six-year-old son Ellis, now entering the first grade.

Your job as mayor has been rough at times, but you still enjoy it. The aspect of the town that has been giving you the most grief recently has been the Maple Island Nuclear Power Plant, the largest industry in Riverton. It produces power for not only Riverton but nearly half of the state also.

Yesterday, you received a letter from your long time friend, Jerry Brown, Vice President of Waste Management for the Maple Island Nuclear Power Plant. He was writing regarding a suggested plan for expanding the waste disposal pools at the plant to accommodate the growing number of used power assemblies.

Today you receive a letter from CAFSE (Citizens Action for a Safe Environment) adamantly opposing not only the expansion of the power plant but also the fact that the plant is operating at all. An open discussion on the proposed expansion has already been slated for next month's town council meeting. You have only five weeks to garner support for whatever position you take.

What do we know?	What do we need to know?	How can we find out?

PROBLEM LOG QUESTIONS

As the problem evolves, keep a list of the issues you think are associated with the original problem statement. Use this list to help organize your thinking and record the connections you are thinking about between the pieces of information or ideas you are developing.

HANDOUT 1.4

PROBLEM LOG QUESTIONS

1. After our first couple of days of discussion, what do you think the problem really is?

   Why do you think this is the main problem?

   Is it the same problem you thought was the main problem when we first started talking?

   If not, how has the problem changed?

   What are the issues you are most interested in finding out about?

   What seems most curious to you?

2. Look at this issue from another viewpoint. What will the similarities of the old and new perspectives be?

   What will the differences be?

HANDOUT 1.5

PROBLEM LOG QUESTIONS

Now that we have created a comprehensive class web of the questions surrounding nuclear energy, create a detailed specific web of questions surrounding the particular topic you want to investigate.

Hot Rods: Nuclear Energy and Nuclear Waste
Supplementary Information for Lesson 1

NOTE TO TEACHER

The majority of the materials presented in this section elaborate on the problem presented in the first edition of the unit. Included are the letters, newspaper articles, a map of Riverton, some general information, descriptions of the Barretts, the Maple Island Nuclear Power Plant, and incidence rates of cancer in Riverton.

If the information seems somewhat disjointed, it is because it was developed to answer specific questions raised by students during the pilot testing of the unit. Assuming that other students will think of similar questions, the materials were included. However, these materials may not answer all of the questions that another creative group of students could imagine. Teachers are encouraged to supplement the story with information of their own making. What is important is that the information presented remains factual, and that the representation of the information be as "authentic" as possible.

Included as supplementary information are the following:

- Additional Information about Riverton

- Riverton Map

- CAFSE Letter to Residents

- Background Notes: ACME Power's Maple Island Nuclear Power Facility

- Cancer Patients in Riverton (1994–1995)

- ACME Power (Office of the Director) Memorandum

- Newspaper Article, "Silent Holocaust"

- CAFSE Newspaper Article

- ACME Power (Department of Waste Management) Memorandum

- City of Riverton Ordinance 829-85 and Amendment

- Memo to the Mayor

Additional Information about Riverton

Background Information: The Barretts and Maple Island

The Barretts have lived in Riverton, Parkland since 1972. Their home is located 5.2 miles from the Maple Island Nuclear Power Plant—the facility which serves as an energy source for the area. In fact, 33% of the energy which supplies the community comes from this facility. The plant was built in 1970 and there have been no problems of which the public has been aware, until now. ACME Power Company owns the Maple Island Nuclear Power Plant. Up to this point, you have tried to balance the different sides of the power plant issue to try to appease as many parties as possible. You realize that whatever decision you make will inevitably upset one of the groups. You thought of "passing the buck" along to the state or U.S. government to make the decision, but the other day there was a message from Congressman Paul Greene, a representative to the U.S. Congress from the local Congressional District. Congressman Greene has received both letters of complaint from CAFSE and letters from power plant workers concerned about losing their jobs. He believes you could better solve this controversy than he could, since you know all the parties involved better than he does.

Riverton Map
1 INCH = 4 MILES

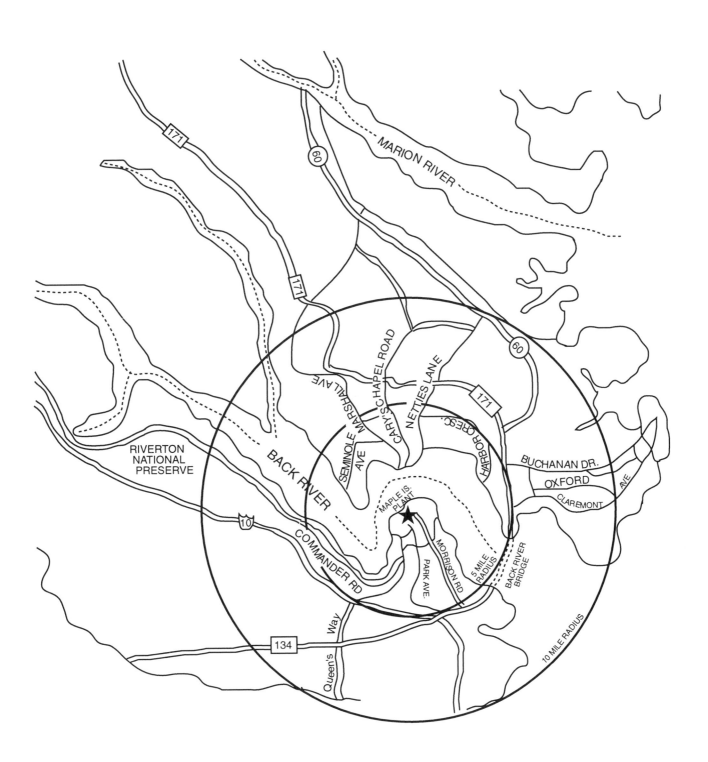

Citizens for a Safe Environment
1234 Jamestown Road
Riverton, Parkland 08934-1882

Dear Resident,

Is our community safe? Towns across the nation are beginning to ask this question. As nuclear power plants proliferate, so do many potential dangers. Our water and our environment are endangered by these facilities, and our health may be too. Incidence of cancer is on the rise in Riverton, especially among our children. Members of Citizens for a Safe Environment (CAFSE) believe that the Maple Island Nuclear Power facility owned by ACME Power is directly related to the increased frequency of the disease. We urge you to join our efforts to CLOSE THE PLANT and make Riverton safe for our children again.

For more information about CAFSE, call Rebecca Weaver at 555-1234.

Sincerely,

CAFSE Membership

Background Notes
ACME Power's Maple Island Nuclear Power Facility

The Maple Island Nuclear Generating Plant in Riverton, Parkland, has two Westinghouse pressurized water reactors which produce nearly 33% of ACME Electric Power Company's electrical power. This nuclear facility originally had 210 fuel assemblies which made up the reactor core; the plant is shut down for refueling approximately every three years. When this refueling occurs, approximately 70 fuel assemblies (one-third of the reactor core) are removed from the reactor and replaced which new fuel assemblies. The spent-fuel assemblies are then moved to the spent-fuel pools for storage.

"Spent fuel" consists of reactor fuel assemblies which have been irradiated in the reactor core until they have been exhausted, or "spent," as a fuel source. These assemblies contain highly radioactive fission products which include uranium, plutonium, strontium-90, iodine, and cesium-137. Each of these by-products is potentially dangerous.

The spent fuel assemblies at the Maple Island nuclear facility are no longer able to sustain normal reactor operation efficiently: thus they must be removed from the reactor. Fissionable materials remain in the spent fuel, and they are capable of maintaining a nuclear reaction. For this reason the ACME Power Company originally planned to send the spent fuel (following short-term on-site storage) to a nuclear fuel repository in order to permanently store it safely.

Two spent-fuel pools were built in order to provide the capacity to safely store 210 fuel assemblies. The smaller pool was intended primarily to handle a spent-fuel shipping cask; the larger of the two pools was designed to store spent nuclear fuel. The racks were constructed so that fuel assemblies are stored vertically, each in its own cavity. It is important that the assemblies be kept far enough apart in order to prevent a sustained nuclear reaction. Since water moderates the hot spent fuel and acts as a shield from radiation, all fuel-handling operations in the pool are performed under water.

In the early 1980's it became apparent that the permanent repository proposed in the Nuclear Waste Policy Act of 1982 would not be fully operational in time to take spent fuel from the Maple Island Plant—so a modification project was initiated in 1985 to increase the pool storage capacity. The new pool layout, which used existing space more efficiently, expanded the capacity from 210 fuel assemblies to 687.

After the modification project, spent-fuel assemblies continued to accumulate in the pool. ACME claims that shutdown of the power plant in inevitable unless the old stainless steel spent-fuel racks are replaced with "absorber" racks which consist of storage cavities whose walls have three layers—a layer of Boraflex (a neutron-absorbing alloy which allows spent-fuel assemblies to be placed closer together) sandwiched between two layers of stainless steel. ACME proposes at this time to enlarge the capacity of the spent-fuel from its current capacity of 687 to a total of 1,582.

The proposed modification will increase the pool storage capacity to the maximum extent within the confines of the existing pool walls. ACME requests approval to carry out this proposal from the Parkland Energy Agency and from the NRC.

Information adapted from: Parisi, Lynn (Ed.). *Hot Rods: Storage of Spent Nuclear Fuel*. Boulder, CO: Social Science Education Consortium, Inc.

Cancer Patients in Riverton (1994–1995)

	Patient and Address	Diagnosis	Age	Date of Diagnosis
1.	Betti Paige McFarlane 106 Park Avenue	Colon Cancer	74	July 1994
2.	Timothy O'Bryan 106 Park Avenue	Stomach Cancer	68	September 1994
3.	Susan Hogge 317 Cedar Lane	Bone Cancer	35	November 1994
4.	Sean Pedersen 215 Catesby Jones Dr.	Myelogenous Leukemia	4	January 1995
5.	Jenny Pedersen 215 Catesby Jones Dr.	Myelogenous Leukemia	6	July 1995
6.	Mathew Jacobs 74 Fern Street	Lung Cancer	49	February 1995
7.	Alyssa Barns 275 Morrison Road	Skin Cancer	19	April 1995
8.	Brian Harper 232 Park Avenue	Prostate Cancer	79	June 1995
9.	Julienne Tipins 36 Nettles Lane	Thyroid Cancer	38	August 1995
10.	David Montgomery 11 Chapel Road	Bone Cancer	57	June 1995
11.	Patricia Higgins 311 Cedar Lane	Breast Cancer	28	September 1994
12.	Mary McClosky 216 Park Avenue	Splenic Cancer	81	August 1995
13.	Janet Segal 12 Fern Street	Bone Cancer	53	July 1995
14.	Paul Miller 300 Park Avenue	Colon Cancer	74	November 1994
15.	Helen Roberts 3 Harbor Crescent	Breast Cancer	48	September 1995
16.	Joanne Marcus 18 Park Avenue	Breast Cancer	72	March 1995
17.	John Gilespi 8 Pine Avenue	Lung Cancer	42	January 1995
18.	Paulette Snyder 275 Morrison Rd.	Leukemia	19	April 1994
19.	Brad Snyder 205 Morrison Rd.	Skin Cancer	38	September 1995
20.	Todd Bristol 15 Park Avenue	Thyroid Nodules	22	December 1994
21.	Jason Knott 112 Park Avenue	Esophageal Cancer	71	February 1995

ACME Power

"Pioneers in the Power Industry"

Office of the Director

Memorandum

To: Public Relations Office

From: Don Feldhouse, Director

Date:

Re: Town Meeting on

These two documents recently came across my desk. It is imperative that the community understand the facts regarding our Maple Island Plant and nuclear power in general before they take action. I would like you to attend the town meeting and be prepared to answer questions regarding how nuclear power is generated, the positive and negative consequences of using nuclear power as well as the consequences of not using nuclear power.

The policy of this company has been to be completely honest in our presentation of information. I firmly believe that the prejudices many people bring to the nuclear power issue is the consequence of inadequate or faulty information. Please be sure that your presentation presents the facts in a fair and unbiased manner in light of our goal of providing a valuable service to the community.

Silent Holocaust

By Eugene McLawhon
Danforth Times News Service

Danforth—The worst accident in the history of the Meadowland weapons complex occurred here on November 15, 1989, when a $40 million blaze was started as plutonium ignited. Immediately after the fire, readings revealed radioactivity more than 200 times higher than the normal background level.

It was soon revealed that the Danforth Nuclear Weapons Power Station raged out of control because simple safety upgrades had not been made due to budget constraints. When close inspection of the facility began, huge drums were found stored on-site which leaked oil contaminated with plutonium.

Since the Manhattan Project of the 1940s, nuclear weapons plants have been supervised by lax government regulations. Documents secured by a Meadowland environmental group under the Freedom of Information Act revealed that between 1958 and 1968 the Danforth plant released small but significant amounts of plutonium into the air every day.

Studies of nearby residents show a higher than average rate of leukemia and other cancers. Toxic wastes and radioactivity have been detected in ponds as well as on nearby property. There is concern by health officials about the safety of water supplies in the area.

The details of mismanagement at the Danforth facility are shocking, yet consistent. Recently, Frank Abney, a Danforth plant worker, revealed in testimony before senate investigators that he had been assured that contamination at the work site was at an "acceptable" level.

He stated that he was never advised as to which radioactive substances to avoid on the site. In April 1989, he discovered he was contaminated with plutonium.

"We are living through a 'Silent Holocaust,' and we're tired of being ignored by our government. It's time we stop remediation—the expensive 'undoing' of mistakes. We must have full-scale prevention. Today, more than ever, the administration must begin a restrained path of self-protection."

CAFSE Newspaper Article

Citizen Action Group Protests Nuclear Power Plant

by Terry Gray
Parkland Times News Service

Riverton—Citizens Action for a Safe Environment (CAFSE), a local environmental group, staged a protest in front of Maple Island Nuclear Power Plant on Friday.

Residents of Riverton, want to shut down the nuclear power plant after a $785,000 campaign by ACME Power Company failed to overcome arguments based less on environmental and safety issues than on economics.

Many of the citizens were convinced that the Maple Island Plant could not provide electricity to their community at a cost lower than other fuels. In 1989, for example, Riverton's electricity cost was more than twice the cost generated by natural gas.

An important consequence of citizen group action in drawing public attention, discussion, a debate concerning the nuclear establishment is to "de-mystify" the processes and human costs of nuclear energy production.

The protest held by CAFSE in Riverton draws focus on other nuclear power facilities in Parkland and throughout the nation. Once touted as the best alternative to oil, nuclear energy's fall from grace began with a nuclear plant disaster at Pennsylvania's Three Mile Island (TMI) in 1979.

Human error as well as equipment failure resulted in the destruction of 70% of TMI's nuclear reactor. Tens of thousands of people were evacuated from the area because of concern over the damaging effect of radioactive emissions released from the plant.

Public confidence in nuclear power was eroded, and the accident resulted in the Nuclear Regulatory Commission's issuing new safety regulations. These anti-nuclear activists declare that no nuclear power plant is completely safe because of the highly radioactive nuclear waste that is a by-product of nuclear power generation.

Others are concerned about the effects of human health and the impact on the individual. CAFSE members point to the possible connection between leukemia and nuclear power emissions.

The CAFSE group has been trying to monitor the incidence of leukemia in the area around the power plant since its opening to determine whether or not nuclear power emissions are a threat to health and life. "Although the data are not absolutely clear, we think there is a link," said one CAFSE advocate.

A mother's perspective sheds another light on the issue. Barbara Anderson is the mother of 16-year-old Alyssa, who has recently been diagnosed as having leukemia.

Nuclear power advocates, however, are determined to turn nuclear energy's bad reputation around in the 1990s. Their renewed efforts have revived the debate over nuclear power's role in America's energy future. Supporters believe that nuclear power is an ideal source of electricity.

They argue that nuclear plants could help reduce America's dependency on foreign oil because uranium ore, the fuel source used in nuclear fission, is widely distributed throughout the United States. They contend that this dependency on foreign oil is brought even more into focus in the wake of the Persian Gulf War. "We've just witnessed the greatest reason for not importing oil," says Janet Alexander, media director of the U.S. Council of Energy Awareness, a pro-nuclear power industry group.

But critics of nuclear power note that only about 5% of U.S. electricity is currently generated by oil today, compared with 18% in 1973. Most oil consumption goes for transportation, not the generation of electricity! Thus, creating more nuclear power plants may produce more electricity, but it would do little to reduce America's dependence on oil.

Nevertheless, proponents of nuclear power claim that oil and coal produce dangerous emissions that pollute the atmosphere. Nuclear energy is a cleaner source of power because it does not emit such gases, they say.

Anti-nuclear activists vehemently disagree. The residents demonstrating in the Citizens Action for a Safe Environment protest are anxious for the Maple Island Nuclear Power Company to get rid of the radioactive waste elsewhere. They fear a "core meltdown" or other tragic accident associated with the nuclear facility.

By focusing attention on the nuclear waste issue, the group plans to expose ACME's possible "covert operations" concerning cover-up of plant problems/accidents for the past years. Their protest heightens public awareness concerning such possibilities.

These citizens recognize that the safe disposal of high-level waste remains a difficult, and perhaps insoluble, problem for the nuclear industry. They are aware that efforts to find a permanent repository for nuclear waste have been fiercely opposed by residents of the areas being considered.

There is a strong cry of "Not in my backyard!" (NIMBY Syndrome) throughout the nation.

Nuclear industry advocates remain optimistic as they point to the Bush administration's recent show of support for nuclear power in its long-awaited national energy strategy. They point out that other nations such as Britain, Japan, Germany, and South Korea rely on nuclear power to supply a significant percentage of their energy production. More than 70% of France's electricity is generated by nuclear power.

Yet, the citizens of Riverton point out in their protest that the possibility of an accident at Maple Island facility is a reality they want to bring to the attention of the public. They point to the accident at Japan's Mihama nuclear power plant of February 9 of this year. This, they say, reminds the public that no country is immune from the threat of nuclear disaster.

ACME Power

"Pioneers in the Power Industry"
Department of Waste Management

Memorandum

To: Office of Mayor Christine Barrett
From: Jerry Brown, Vice President of Waste Management
Date:
Re: Expanding Waste Disposal Capacity

We at the Maple Island Nuclear Power Plant foresee the need to expand our on-site waste disposal capacity in the near future. In the past there has been much discussion and opposition to expanding our waste storage facilities. For your information, I have provided a short history of our waste disposal capabilities.

When the Maple Island Nuclear Power Plant was constructed in 1970, ACME Power Company intended to store spent nuclear fuel "on-site" until a permanent repository was provided by the U.S. Department of Energy. Initially, two spent-fuel pools provided the capacity to store 210 fuel assemblies. In the mid-1980's it became apparent that the repository proposed by the U.S. Department of Energy in the Nuclear Waste Policy Act of 1982 would not be operational in time to dispose of the spent fuel from the Maple Island plant. Consequently, a modification project was initiated in 1984 to increase the pool storage capacity from 210 fuel assemblies to 678 assemblies. Now we see the need to expand the capacity to 1,582 assemblies to keep the plant operational.

Due to Local Ordinance 829-85, we need to gain the approval of the Mayor and Council before implementing any new expansion or addition of waste facilities within the jurisdiction of the City of Riverton. We ask for your approval in a timely fashion. Thank you.

The City of Riverton

City of Good Tidings
Office of the Mayor

Local Ordinance 829-85 (adopted August 15, 1985):

All businesses, industries, nonprofit organizations, and/or living complexes must apply for approval through the Mayor's office before beginning any expansions, additions, or formations of waste disposal sites within the jurisdiction of the City of Riverton. This includes garbage disposal, human waste, hospital waste, low and high grade nuclear waste, and any other waste products known to be hazardous or potentially hazardous to the citizens of Riverton. Failure to comply could result in fines of a minimum of $1,000 with no upper limit.

Amendment to Local Ordinance 829-85 (adopted September 15, 1987):

In addition to the pre-set conditions to L.O. 829-85, the parties responsible for obtaining permission are extended to include local, state, and federal government agencies, as well as religious institutions and school districts. The town council has the right to call for a special review of any request accepted or denied by the Mayor regarding L.O. 829-85.

To: Mayor Christine Barrett
From: Congressman Paul Greene
Date:
Subject: **Maple Island Power Plant**

I have received letters from your environmental group, CAFSE, complaining about safety concerns at Maple Island. However, I have also received letters from power plant employees who are concerned about losing their jobs.

I think you can resolve this controversy better than I can, since you are closer to all the parties involved and the data from the plant. I will support your decision at the national level.

Lesson

Nuclear Power
Plants as "Systems"

LESSON LENGTH: 1 session

INSTRUCTIONAL PURPOSE

- To allow students to identify and define the parts of a system.

MATERIALS AND HANDOUTS

Resource Materials on nuclear power plants, in particular, "Our Electric Future" in *National Geographic,* August 1991, pp. 60–89.

Handout 2.1: Systems Parts Chart
Handout 2.2: Problem Log Questions
Handout 2.3: Problem Log Questions

THINGS TO DO

1. Investigate the workings of a typical nuclear power plant. See the *National Geographic* article cited above. (If information from a local plant site is available, then utilize that resource.)

2. Describe the concept of systems to students. Introduce students to the terms associated with systems. Have students derive or find definitions for each term:

   boundary: sets what is inside the system and what is outside the system

   elements: the parts that make up the system

   input: anything that goes into the system from outside the system

   output: anything that the system releases to the outside world

   interactions: the effects the parts of the system have on each other

3. Elicit examples of systems that students are familiar with (e.g., circulation system, school system). Have them identify and discuss the parts of those systems.

4. Discuss how a nuclear power plant could be considered a system.

5. Have students complete a Systems Parts Chart (Handout 2.1) for nuclear power plants.

6. Have students complete Problem Logs (Handouts 2.2 and 2.3).

THINGS TO ASK

- Why might it be important to understand the nuclear power plant in terms of a "system"?

- How could thinking about systems help you organize your thoughts about the problem here?

- How could using systems help you explain the problem to other people?

- What specific information about systems ought to be presented at the Town Meeting?

- How could the topic you're investigating be seen as a system?

- Do all electric power plants have the same system? Why?

- What makes nuclear power plants unique?

- What other systems are we working with in this problem?

- Could the town be considered as a system? Could a nuclear reaction be considered a system?

ASSESSMENT

1. Completion of Systems Parts Chart.
2. Problem Log Questions.

EXTENSION ACTIVITIES

Have students build a model of a nuclear power plant facility marking inputs, outputs, etc.

HANDOUT 2.1

SYSTEMS PARTS CHART

1. What are the boundaries of the system? Why did you choose them? Were there other possibilities?

2. List some important elements of the system.

3. Describe input into the system. Where does it come from?

4. Describe output from the system. What part(s) of the system produce it?

5. Describe some important interactions:
   a. among system elements

   b. between system elements and input into the system

6. What would happen to the system if the interactions in 5a could not take place? In 5b?

PROBLEM LOG QUESTIONS

1. Describe how your classroom can be considered a system. Identify the following system components:

   boundaries:

   elements:

   inputs:

   outputs:

   interactions:

2. Assume that your classroom gets a new computer with access to the Internet. How would this affect the components of the classroom system?

HANDOUT 2.3

PROBLEM LOG QUESTIONS

Look at our large class web of nuclear energy issues. Use a marker to outline any parts of the web that can be considered a system (use a different color marker for each system). Use a different color marker to connect systems to other systems with which they interact.

lesson

3

An Inside Look at Nuclear Power Plants

LESSON LENGTH: 2 sessions

INSTRUCTIONAL PURPOSE

- To provide an opportunity for students to visit a nuclear power facility. (See Optional Lesson #3 on page 67 for possible alternative.)

Session 1

THINGS TO DO

1. Review the "Need to Know" board for questions that still need to be answered.

2. Brainstorm a list of questions students would like to have answered on the field trip.

3. Assign responsibilities for attending to the specifics of different kinds of information to different students.

4. Ask students for a list of things they particularly want to see if it is possible.

THINGS TO ASK

- What questions would you like answered during our field trip?

- Can you think of specific things an energy consultant would look for or ask?

- What about an anti-nuclear activist?

- What should you be looking for or asking of the people at the plant?

- How can we ask these questions in non-offensive ways?

Session 2

THINGS TO DO

1. Students visit a local nuclear power plant.

2. Debrief the field trip. Review the "Need to Know" board, removing questions which have been answered and adding new issues, if necessary. Synthesize new information with current database.

3. Have students complete Problem Log Questions (Handouts 3.2 and 3.3).

ASSESSMENT

1. Evidence of information which students acquired during the field trip.

2. Quality of questions asked while at the site.

Optional lesson

3

Guest Speaker on Nuclear Power

LESSON LENGTH: 3 sessions

INSTRUCTIONAL PURPOSE

- To engage a speaker involved with nuclear power to come to talk to the class, **if a visit to a power plant is not possible.**
- To facilitate students' preparation for the visitor.

MATERIALS AND HANDOUTS

Chart and markers

Audio-Visual equipment for guest speaker

Handout 3.1: Visitor Planning Sheet
Handout 3.2: Problem Log Questions
Handout 3.3: Problem Log Questions

Session 1

THINGS TO DO

1. Help students select which items from the "Need to Know" board might be best answered by the guest speaker. Brainstorm other questions. (The "best" questions to ask will, of course, depend on the area of expertise of the guest speaker.)

2. Sort questions into Most and Least important. Students should also be encouraged to think about the best way to phrase the questions. Are they specific enough? Are they too specific? A core list of questions can be recorded on a chart or on the board. Students can then add any of their own questions to individual Visitor Planning Sheets (Handout 3.1).

THINGS TO ASK

- What information do we want to know about the nuclear power system?

- What information will the guest speaker be most qualified to give?

- What do we want to know by the time the guest speaker leaves?

- What facts do we want to get from this person that might help us with the Maple Island problem?

- Which of these questions are most important?

- How can we get an idea of this person's perspective on this kind of situation?

- Do you think this person will have a bias? What would it be? How can we find out?

Session 2

THINGS TO DO

Guest Speaker: The guest provides his/her information about nuclear power. Students take notes and ask their questions to the guest speaker. Students should also be prepared to share with the guest speaker background on the problem and their actions to date.

Session 3

THINGS TO DO

1. Analyze the guest speaker's information. In a follow-up to the guest speaker, teacher and students should review the "Need to Know" board, removing questions which have been answered and adding new issues, if necessary. Synthesize new information with current data base.

2. Teachers and students should discuss the potential bias in the information provided by the guest speaker and the possible effects of that bias on the validity of the information.

THINGS TO ASK

- What were the things we learned from the guest speaker?
- How does the new information affect our thinking about the problem?
- Do we need to reorganize our approach to the problem?
- Did this person reveal a particular bias? If so, what?
- Where can we go to get another perspective? A balanced report of information?

ASSESSMENT

1. Record of new information in problem logs based on the guest speaker's presentation.
2. Reflection on bias in the problem log.
3. Thank you letter to the guest speaker, detailing which information was particularly helpful.

HANDOUT 3.1
VISITOR PLANNING SHEET

Student Name _____

Name of Visitor _____

Who is this visitor?

_____

_____

_____

Why is this visitor coming to see us?

_____

_____

Why is this visitor important to us?

_____

_____

_____

What would you like to tell our visitor about our problem?

_____

_____

What questions do you want to ask the visitor?

_____

_____

_____

Can bias be prevented or is a person always biased to some degree? What strategies do you think would be helpful to offset our own biases?

Take just a minute to think about the problem itself. What does the problem look like now compared to what it was at the beginning of this segment? How has it changed? What has surprised you about this problem?

Nuclear Reactions

LESSON LENGTH: 3 sessions

INSTRUCTIONAL PURPOSE

- To introduce experimental design in a relevant context.
- To introduce the nuclear fission process and explain how the process generates energy.
- To introduce radioisotopes and radioactive decay (alpha, beta, and gamma decay).
- To allow students to construct a mental model of a chain reaction.

MATERIALS AND HANDOUTS

Periodic Chart of the Elements
100 or more dominoes
Large table or floor space
Stopwatch

Handout 4.1: Nuclear Fission
Handout 4.2: Nuclear Decay Discussion Questions
Handout 4.3: Problem Log Questions
Handout 4.4: Student Brainstorming Worksheet
Handout 4.5: Student Experiment Worksheet
Handout 4.6: Student Protocol Worksheet
Handout 4.7: Laboratory Report Form
Handout 4.8: Sample Protocol Problem Log Questions
Handout 4.9: Problem Log Questions
Handout 4.10: Ping-Pong Decay Worksheet
Handout 4.11: Teacher Ping-Pong Decay Worksheet
Handout 4.12: Problem Log Questions

Session 1

THINGS TO DO

1. Break the class into small groups and pass out Handout 4.1 on nuclear fission. Have students read the information, individually respond to the short answer questions, and discuss their answers within their group. Make sure each group comes to a consensus on each question.

2. Bring class back into the large group and process the question in relation to the "Need to Know" board and Nuclear Power Web.

3. Talk about radiation and what forms it might take. Discuss radioactive decay in terms of the problem. Be sure to mention half-life and disposal of waste materials.

4. Have the students postulate what happens to the stable uranium-238 during nuclear power production. Does it remain unchanged?

5. Once again, break the class into small groups and pass out Handout 4.2 on nuclear decay. Discuss questions and have them read the passage and analyze the decay reactions that follow.

6. Bring class back into the large group to process the connections between "Need to Know" board, Nuclear Power Web, and the discussion.

7. Have students complete Problem Log Questions (Handout 4.3).

THINGS TO ASK

- What is the importance of fission to the nuclear power plant?

- What do we know about fission?

- What have we found out about fission as it relates to power production?

- What is radioactive decay? How does it relate to our problem?

- Are there many types of radioactive decay?

- What is the importance of radioactive decay to our problem?

ASSESSMENT

1. Problem Log Questions
2. Small group discussion handouts

EXTENSIONS

Discuss nuclear fusion and how the sun produces nuclear energy.

Session 2

THINGS TO DO

1. Review the "Need to Know" board and the Nuclear Energy Web and discuss nuclear chain reactions. Certainly nuclear chain reactions are an important consideration in power plant design as well as in the safe handling of any radioactive substance.

2. Talk about ways to show how nuclear chain reactions work. Discuss how transmission of a disease can be seen as a chain reaction. Use the following example.

SCENARIO STATEMENT

Imagine that you come to school one day with a common cold. That day you transmit your cold germs to two other people; they in turn give it to two others; who in turn do the same. Before you know it, everyone in school is sneezing. You have set off a chain reaction. Similarly, electrons in a photomultiplier tube in an electronic instrument multiply in a chain reaction so that a tiny input produces a huge output. When one neutron triggers the release of two or more neutrons in a piece of uranium and the triggered neutrons trigger others in a chain reaction, the results can be devastating.

3. Show students the materials for the lesson. Break students into small groups and ask them to come up with a method for modeling the rates of chain reactions using dominoes. To prompt students for the brainstorming activity, refer to the questions in the following Things to Ask section. Pass out a copy of the Student Brainstorming Worksheet (Handout 4.4) and have them fill it out.

4. Discuss the brainstorming results as a class.

5. Pass out copies of the Student Experiment Worksheet (Handout 4.5). If this is the first time students have seen it, have the class fill it out together and explain the meaning of each of the terms.

6. After they have filled out the Student Experiment Worksheet (Handout 4.5), have each group write their protocol on the Student Protocol Worksheet (Handout 4.6). They should include every step they plan to take, the materials they will use, and a data table to record their data. Students should also indicate what safety procedures they plan to use as a part of the overall experimental design.

7. Have students either work individually or in small groups to conduct the experiment. When they have finished, have them complete the Laboratory Report Form (Handout 4.7).

8. After students perform their experiments, bring the group together to discuss their results, limitations of the results, and possible revisions in experimental design. Complete Handout 4.8 or a version that matches the experiment that students did.

9. Have students complete Handout 4.9, Problem Log Questions.

Sample Protocol

Step #1. Set up a string of dominoes, about half a domino length apart in a straight line. Push the first domino, and measure how long it takes for the entire string to fall over using the stopwatch.

Step #2. Do it again! Arrange an equal number of dominoes in a straight line about half a domino apart. Push the first domino over and calculate the rate at which the dominoes fall. Is this rate constant over time?

Step #3. Next, arrange the same number of dominoes in a pattern as shown in Figure 1. Push the first domino, and measure how long it takes for the entire string to fall over using the stop watch. Compare the length of time needed in this configuration to the length of time needed for the configuration in Step #1.

Step #4. Once again, arrange the dominoes in a pattern as shown in Figure 1. Push the first domino over to calculate the rate at which the dominoes fall. To do this, have one student run the stopwatch and call out the seconds. Other students mark down which row of dominoes fell when the second is called out. The rate can be calculated by counting the number of dominoes that fell during each second separately. How do the rates in Step #2 compare to the rates found in this step?

Figure 1: *Overhead View of Domino Arrangement*

Each row of dominoes is spaced about half a domino length apart just as in Step #1.

NOTE: Arrange the same number of dominoes in the pyramid pattern shown to the left as arranged in the straight line in Step #1 and Step #2. For example, if 100 dominoes are set up in a straight line in Step #1 and #2, then set up 100 dominoes in the pyramid pattern shown for Step #3 and #4.

THINGS TO ASK

- What do you think a chain reaction is?
- How could you demonstrate this with dominoes?
- Would the rate of the reaction change if we change the spacing between dominoes?
- Would the rate of the reaction change if we change the arrangement of dominoes?

ASSESSMENT

1. Complete Problem Logs
2. Complete Laboratory Report Forms
3. Complete Sample Protocol Problem Log Questions

EXTENSIONS

1. How do nuclear bombs differ from nuclear reactors?
2. What makes a nuclear bomb so powerful?

Session 3

THINGS TO DO

1. At a time when students have begun to investigate radioactive decay, gather them together and have students summarize what they have learned.

2. Tell students that there is an important radioactive decay process that is the basis for nuclear power plant operations, namely:

$$_{92}U^{235} + n \longrightarrow {}_{36}Kr^{90} + {}_{56}Ba^{142} + 4\,n$$

Since four neutrons are released for every neutron consumed, the reaction is self-sustaining—it begins with a single neutron, which reacts and produces four neutrons, which react and produce sixteen, etc.

3. Ask them to imagine the following: (a model originally suggested by Richard P. Feynman, a noted physicist):

> Think of each unstable uranium-235 atom as a mousetrap that has been set with a ping-pong ball balanced on top. If the mousetrap is sprung, the ping-pong ball will fly off: the ping-pong ball acts like the neutron that is released during radioactive decay. (Obviously, this is not a perfectly homologous picture—but it's hard to imagine a mousetrap with four ping-pong balls balanced on top . . .)

Once they have this mental picture, break them into small groups and ask them to fill out the Ping-Pong Decay Worksheet (Handout 4.10).

4. After discussion of Handout 4.10, have students complete Problem Log Questions (Handout 4.12).

ASSESSMENT

Ping-Pong Decay Worksheet

EXTENSIONS

Students could either set this up as a physical model, or write a computer program to model this process.

HANDOUT 4.1

NUCLEAR FISSION

When an atom of the radioactive isotope uranium-235 is bombarded by neutrons, it is possible for the atomic nucleus to absorb one of the "incoming" neutrons. The resultant, and highly unstable uranium-236 nucleus tends to split (hence nuclear fission) forming the nuclei of two new elements—barium and krypton for example—at the same time releasing two or three high energy neutrons, and a large amount of energy (approximately 300 billion joules). If this process is controlled so that one of the released neutrons itself bombards and is absorbed by another uranium-235 nucleus, a chain reaction results which can produce large amounts of energy converted as heat.

This is exactly what happens inside a nuclear reactor. Naturally occurring uranium contains about 99.3% of stable uranium-238, and 0.7% of radioactive uranium-235, a mixture which will not sustain a chain reaction. U-235 can be enriched however, so that the fuel rods in a nuclear reactor contain 97% of U-238 and 3% of U-235. These fuel rods are sheathed in graphite to slow down the movement of the bombarding neutrons, thereby increasing the chances of absorption of neutrons by the U-235 nuclei. In addition, rods of boron steel can be lowered into the reactor to absorb neutrons if the reaction is proceeding too fast.

1. Are all the 300 billion joules produced by a *single* fission reaction converted into heat? What forms could the emergent energy take? Explain your answer.

2. What possible explanations are there for the reason why naturally occurring uranium does *not* produce nuclear chain reactions?

3. What reasons can you give for slowing neutrons down to allow for better absorption rates?

4. What are the possible outcomes of a nuclear reactor that is proceeding too fast and is *not* checked by the boron steel?

Directions: *Read the passage below and respond collaboratively on the questions. Refer to the periodic chart of the elements when necessary.*

In decaying, an isotope may:

- Lose positively charged particles from the atomic nuclei (alpha particles). Because of the resulting loss of atomic mass, this has the effect of converting the original element into one which is placed earlier in the periodic table. An example of alpha-decay is the natural decay of uranium, which through a number of conversions, eventually decays to form lead.

- Lose negatively charged electrons (beta particles). This occurs as the result of a nuclear neutron becoming a proton, and the effect is to move the element "up" the periodic table. An example of beta-decay is the decay of carbon-14 to nitrogen, a process which takes many thousands of years, and which is used in the accurate dating of organic remains.

- Emit, as high energy electromagnetic waves, the highly penetrating (and therefore potentially damaging) gamma rays, which have no electric charge.

1. Analyze the following decay reaction:

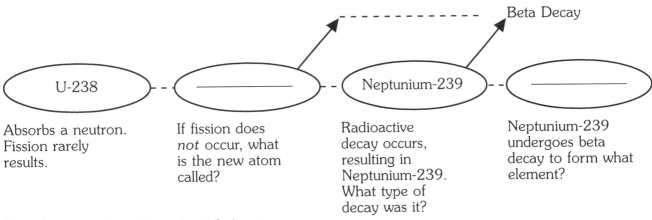

The above reaction takes about 2 days to occur.

2. Analyze the following decay reaction:

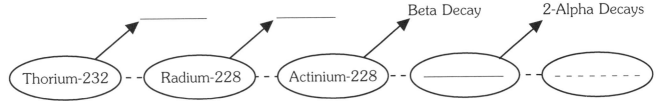

3. What implications does this have on radioactive waste from a nuclear reaction, if any?

ANSWER PROTOCOL FOR HANDOUT 4.2
NUCLEAR DECAY DISCUSSION QUESTIONS

Directions: *Read the passage below and respond collaboratively on the questions. Refer to the periodic chart of the elements when necessary.*

In decaying, an isotope may:

- Lose positively charged particles from the atomic nuclei (alpha particles). Because of the resulting loss of atomic mass, this has the effect of converting the original element into one which is placed earlier in the periodic table. An example of alpha-decay is the natural decay of uranium, which through a number of conversions, eventually decays to form lead.

- Lose negatively charged electrons (beta particles). This occurs as the result of a nuclear neutron becoming a proton, and the effect is to move the element "up" the periodic table. An example of beta-decay is the decay of carbon-14 to nitrogen, a process which takes many thousands of years, and which is used in the accurate dating of organic remains.

- Emit, as high energy electromagnetic waves, the highly penetrating (and therefore potentially damaging) gamma rays, which have no electric charge.

1. Analyze the following decay reaction:

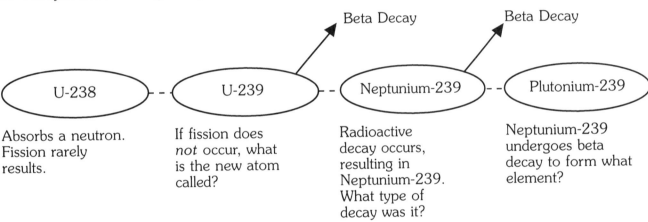

Absorbs a neutron. Fission rarely results.

If fission does *not* occur, what is the new atom called?

Radioactive decay occurs, resulting in Neptunium-239. What type of decay was it?

Neptunium-239 undergoes beta decay to form what element?

The above reaction takes about 2 days to occur.

2. Analyze the following decay reaction:

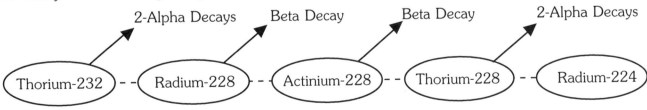

3. What implications does this have on radioactive waste from a nuclear reaction, if any?

87

HANDOUT 4.3

PROBLEM LOG QUESTIONS

1. Discuss the impact of nuclear fission on all the other major parts of the Nuclear Power Web.

2. Discuss the impact radioactive decay has on the other major parts of the Nuclear Power Web.

3. How do these two properties, fission and decay, alter, change, or modify the overall problem? How has your outlook on the problem changed as a result of an examination of fission and decay?

HANDOUT 4.4

STUDENT BRAINSTORMING WORKSHEET

1. What do we need to find out? (What is the scientific problem?)

2. What materials do we have available?

3. How can we use these materials to help us find out?

4. What do we think will happen? (What is our hypothesis?)

5. What will we need to observe or measure in order to find out the answer to our scientific question?

Adapted from Cothron, J. G., Giese, R. N., & Rezba, R. J. (1989). *Students and research*. Dubuque, IA: Kendall/Hunt Publishing Co.

Title of Experiment:

Hypothesis (Educated guess about what will happen):

Independent Variable (The variable that **you change**):

Dependent Variable (The variable that responds to changes in the independent variable):

Observations/Measurements to Make:

Constants (All the things or factors that remain the same):

Control (The standard for comparing experimental effects):

1. List the materials you will need.

2. Write a step-by-step description of what you will do (like a recipe!). List every action you will take during the experiment.

3. What data will you be collecting?

4. Design a data table to collect and analyze your information.

HANDOUT 4.7

LABORATORY REPORT FORM

1. What did you do or test? (Include your experiment title.)

2. How did you do it? Cite materials and methods. You can go back to your Student Protocol Worksheet (Handout 4.6) and use the information from the first two questions.

3. What did you find out? (Include a data summary and the explanation of its meaning.)

4. What did you learn from your experiment?

5. What further questions do you now have?

6. Does the information you learned help with the problem?

SAMPLE PROTOCOL PROBLEM LOG QUESTIONS

1. Which reaction set up took a shorter time to knock over all the dominoes? Why?

2. Describe how the number of dominoes being knocked over per second change in each reaction type.

3. Imagine that the dominoes are neutrons released by uranium atoms when they fission. Neutrons from the nucleus of each fissioning uranium atom hit other uranium atoms and cause them to fission. In a complete paragraph, compare and contrast the domino reactions to a nuclear chain reaction.

1. How has the problem changed now that you have developed an idea of a chain reaction?

2. What impact do chain reactions have on the overall problem and the Nuclear Power Web?

3. What do you think is the next step in addressing the problem? Why?

HANDOUT 4.10

PING-PONG DECAY WORKSHEET

1. What would happen if you had a single ping-pong ball-mousetrap combination set up in the middle of an otherwise empty room and it spontaneously "decayed," releasing its ping-pong ball at high speed?

2. What if you had a single ping-pong ball-mousetrap setup in the middle of a group of unset, ordinary mousetraps and it suddenly "decayed"?

3. What would happen if you had a room full of ping-pong ball-mousetrap setups placed at one foot intervals and one of them spontaneously "decayed," releasing its ping-pong ball at high speed?

4. Which of the three experiments described in question #1 through question #3 is a good model for a nuclear chain reaction? Why?

5. "Critical mass" is the term that describes the smallest amount of a radioactive material needed to set off a spontaneous chain reaction. How could you find out what the critical mass of ping-pong ball-mousetrap setups would be? What factors would you have to consider?

6. Critical density is the fraction of the atoms that need to be unstable in order for the material to be able to sustain a chain reaction. How could you use the ping-pong ball-mousetrap setup to model critical density?

7. Moderators are substances that absorb neutrons and prevent them from causing any more radioactive decays. How could you model the action of a moderator in the ping-pong ball-mousetrap experiment?

HANDOUT 4.11

TEACHER PING-PONG DECAY WORKSHEET

1. What would happen if you had a single ping-pong ball-mousetrap combination set up in the middle of an otherwise empty room and it spontaneously "decayed," releasing its ping-pong ball at high speed?

    (Answer: You'd have a sprung mousetrap and a ping-pong ball.)

2. What if you had a single ping-pong ball-mousetrap setup in the middle of a group of unset, ordinary mousetraps and it suddenly "decayed"?

    (Answer: you'd have one more sprung mousetrap to add to the collection, plus a bouncing ping-pong ball that would eventually come to rest.)

3. What would happen if you had a room full of ping-pong ball-mousetrap setups placed at one foot intervals and one of them spontaneously "decayed," releasing its ping-pong ball at high speed?

    (Answer: The first ping-pong ball would probably bounce onto another setup, causing it to decay. This process would repeat itself and you would have a chain reaction that would result in the decay of most (if not all) of the setups in the room.)

4. Which of the three experiments described in questions #1–#3 is a good model for a nuclear chain reaction? Why?

    (Answer: #3)

5. "Critical mass" is the term that describes the smallest amount of a radioactive material needed to set off a spontaneous chain reaction. How could you find out what the critical mass of ping-pong ball-mousetrap setups would be? What factors would you have to consider?

    (Answer: You'd have to test and see. Factors to consider would be the hardness of the floor and walls, which would affect the ability of the balls to bounce; the existence or nonexistence of floors and ceiling; the shape of the array of mousetraps; the spacing of the mousetraps from each other; the number of ping-pong balls released as each setup decays . . . and so on . . .)

6. Critical density is the fraction of the atoms that need to be unstable in order for the material to be able to sustain a chain reaction. How could you use the ping-pong ball-mousetrap setup to model critical density?

   (Answer: You could model it experimentally, using a combination of sprung mouse-traps and ping-pong ball setups and gradually increasing the number of setups.)

7. Moderators are substances that absorb neutrons and prevent them from causing any more radioactive decays. How could you model the action of a moderator in the ping-pong ball-mousetrap experiment?

   (Answer: One way would be to add boxes full of something that would stop ping-pong balls that landed in them from bouncing. Enough of these boxes spaced at regular intervals should be able to reduce the intensity of the chain reaction or stop it altogether.)

PROBLEM LOG QUESTIONS

1. Think about what you have learned about systems and apply that knowledge to nuclear reactions.

2. What systems are involved in nuclear reactions?

3. Draw a diagram of one of the systems within nuclear reactions. Label all parts of the system in terms of its boundary, elements, input, output, and interactions:

4. What safety issues emerge when you think of your nuclear system interactions?

Half-Life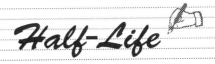

LESSON LENGTH: 3 sessions—1 session each for planning, exercises, and discussion.

INSTRUCTIONAL PURPOSE

- To develop a physical understanding of half-life through an activity and a conceptual understanding of half-life as it pertains to radioactive materials.

MATERIALS AND HANDOUTS

One shoe box per group

200 or more pennies per group

200 or more brass paper fasteners per group

200 or more six-sided dice per group

Three sheets of graph paper per person

Optional: Graphing could be performed by using a computerized graphing program.

Handout 5.1: Student Brainstorming Worksheet

Handout 5.2: Student Experiment Worksheet

Handout 5.3: Student Protocol Worksheet

Handout 5.4: Laboratory Report Form

Handout 5.5: Sample Problem Log Questions

Handout 5.6: Problem Log Questions

Handout 5.7: Data Tables

Handout 5.8: Discussion Questions

Handout 5.9: Decay Products of Radioisotopes

Handout 5.10: Challenge Questions

Sessions 1–2

THINGS TO DO

1. Review the "Need to Know" board and the Nuclear Energy Web and discuss why half-life would be an important concept to understand and explain at the town meeting. Certainly half-life is an important consideration in the safe handling of any radioactive substance.

2. Talk about ways to test half-life of radioactive materials. Discuss half-life in terms other than radioactive materials.

   Many things grow at a fairly steady rate: population, money in the bank, and the thickness of paper that is continuously folded over onto itself. Many other things decrease at a steady rate: the value of money in the bank, the amount of vacant area in a place where population is growing, and the amount of material undergoing radioactive decay. Radioactive materials become less radioactive over time as a result of a process known as radioactive decay. An understanding of radioactive decay is essential to an understanding of the plans for permanent disposal of radioactive wastes. A useful way to describe the rate of decrease is in terms of *half-life—the time it takes for the quantity of material to reduce to half its initial value.* For steady decrease, called exponential decrease, the half-life always stays the same. Radioactive materials are characterized by their rates of decay and are rated in terms of their half-lives.

3. Show students the materials for the lesson. Tell the students that they will be using these materials to simulate half-life. You may use the following rules for "decay" of each of the materials:

   - pennies: eliminate all that land heads up
   - brass fasteners: eliminate the ones that land on their heads
   - dice: eliminate those that land with the one's side up

   Break students into small groups and ask them to come up with a method for measuring half-life of various substances using the materials available. Pass out a copy of the Student Brainstorming Worksheet (Handout 5.1) and have them fill it out. To prompt student brainstorming, refer to the questions in the Things to Ask section to follow.

4. Discuss the brainstorming results as a class.

5. Pass out copies of the Student Experiment Worksheet (Handout 5.2). If this is the first time students have seen it, have the class fill it out together and explain the meaning of each of the terms.

110

6. After they have filled out the Student Experiment Worksheet (Handout 5.2), have each group write their experiment protocol on the Student Protocol Worksheet (Handout 5.3). (See the Sample Experiment Protocol as an example of the experimental procedure students might develop.) They should include every step they plan to take, the materials they will use, and a data table (Handout 5.7 reflects a sample data table that may be used) to record their data. Students should also indicate what safety procedures they plan to use as a part of the overall experimental design.

7. Have students come together as a class and reach a consenses on an experiment protocol.

8. The class should be separated into groups of 2–4 students depending upon the availability of materials for each group. If the availability of materials is problematic, have the groups share the materials by setting up work stations; one with a shoe box and pennies, another with a shoe box and dice, and a third with a shoe box and brass fasteners.

9. After students perform their experiments have them complete Handout 5.4. Bring the group together to discuss their results, limitations of the results, and possible revisions in experimental design.

10. Have students complete Handout 5.5.

11. Discuss answers to questions #1–#5 on Handout 5.5. Then have students complete Problem Log Questions (Handout 5.6).

NOTE TO TEACHER

The questions in Handout 5.5 reflect the use of the sample experiment protocol. This handout should be modified to reflect the experimental protocol developed by the students. If you try the experiment in advance, the range of answers for Handout 5.5 will be readily apparent.

THINGS TO ASK

- What do you think half-life is in terms of radioactive materials?

- How could we demonstrate half-life with these materials?

- Will the half-lives be different for the different materials?

- What characteristics about the materials will determine their individual half-lives?

ASSESSMENT

1. Problem Log Questions.
2. Protocol Worksheet.

Session 3

PURPOSE

This lesson will clarify that radioactive materials lose their radioactivity over time through the process of radioactive decay. Additionally, students will learn that the time for radioactive materials to lose essentially all their radioactivity can vary from seconds to thousands of years. The half-life of a radioisotope is the time it takes for a quantity of radioisotope to lose half of its present radioactivity. The necessity of providing safe disposal of radioactive wastes will be discussed.

THINGS TO DO

1. Discuss the students' answers to question #6 of the half-life activity in Handout 5.5. *(Compare and contrast the usefulness of knowing the half-life of pennies, dice, and/or brass fasteners to the usefulness of knowing the half-life of radioactive waste.)*

2. Break the class into small groups and distribute Handout 5.8 for discussion. They are to cooperatively fill in the chart and answer the discussion questions.

3. Bring the class back into the large group to share answers.

4. Again, break the class into small groups and disperse Handout 5.9 on radioactive decay products. Have the students collaboratively answer and discuss the attached questions.

5. Bring the class back together into the large group and discuss each group's conclusions.

THINGS TO ASK

- Describe the similarities and differences between the half-life activity from the previous session and the half-life of radioactive substances.

- Do you think it would be possible to predict when a radioisotope will decay and produce radiation? Why? Why not?

- After a radioisotope decays, is it necessarily stable and nonradioactive?

- Discuss the meaning of the term "decay chain"?

- What are the implications for proper waste disposal for radioisotopes that do not decay into stable substances?

- What do you think is the relationship, if any, between how intense the radioactivity of a radioisotope and its half-life?

ASSESSMENT

1. Half-life activity sheets.
2. Use of the Handout 5.10 as reinforcement/homework to assess student learning.

HANDOUT 5.1

STUDENT BRAINSTORMING WORKSHEET

1. What do we need to find out? (What is the scientific problem?)

2. What materials do we have available?

3. How can we use these materials to help us find out?

4. What do we think will happen? (What is our hypothesis?)

5. What will we need to observe or measure in order to find out the answer to our scientific question?

Adapted from Cothron, J. G., Giese, R. N., & Rezba, R. J. (1989). *Students and research*. Dubuque, IA: Kendall/Hunt Publishing Co.

HANDOUT 5.2

STUDENT EXPERIMENT WORKSHEET

Title of Experiment:

Hypothesis (Educated guess about what will happen):

Independent Variable (The variable that **you change**):

Dependent Variable (The variable that responds to changes in the independent variable):

Observations/Measurements to Make:

Constants (All the things or factors that remain the same):

Control (The standard for comparing experimental effects):

HANDOUT 5.3

STUDENT PROTOCOL WORKSHEET

1. List the materials you will need.

2. Write a step-by-step description of what you will do (like a recipe!). List every action you will take during the experiment.

3. What data will you be collecting?

4. Design a data table to collect and analyze your information.

Sample Experiment Protocol

PROCEDURE

If it is not possible to obtain enough materials for each group, arrange the materials in stations about the room. Station #1 will have a shoe box and pennies, station #2 will have a shoe box and dice, and station #3 will have a shoe box and brass fasteners. Allow each group to take turns collecting data from each station.

1. Place the pennies in a shoe box, and place the lid on the box. Shake the box for several seconds. Open the box and remove all the pennies that are heads up. Count these, and record the number in Data Table A (see Handout 5.7 as an example). Do not put the removed pennies back in the box.

2. Repeat Step 1 over and over until one or no pennies remain in the box. Record the number of pennies removed during each trial in Data Table A.

3. Calculate the number of pennies remaining after each shake by subtracting the number of pennies removed each time from the previous number remaining, and record in Data Table A.

4. Graph the number of pennies remaining after each shake (vertical axis) versus the number of shakes (horizontal axis). Draw a smooth line that best fits the points.

5. Repeat steps 1–5, but substitute the six-sided dice for the pennies. After each thorough shake, remove die with the one's side up. Record information on Data Table B.

6. Repeat steps 1–5, but substitute the brass fasteners for the pennies. After each thorough shake, dump the brass fasteners out of the box onto the table. Remove all the brass fasteners that stand on their heads, as you did for the pennies that were heads up. Place the rest of the brass fasteners back into the box and continue as stated above. Record information on Data Table C.

HANDOUT 5.4

LABORATORY REPORT FORM

1. What did you do or test? (Include your experiment title.)

2. How did you do it? Cite materials and methods. You can go back to your Student Protocol Worksheet (Handout 5.3) and use the information from the first two questions.

3. What did you find out? (Include a data summary and the explanation of its meaning.)

4. What did you learn from your experiment?

5. What further questions do you now have?

6. Does the information you learned help with the problem?

SAMPLE PROBLEM LOG QUESTIONS

(BASED ON THE SAMPLE EXPERIMENT PROTOCOL)

1. What does each graph represent?

2. Approximately what percentage of the remaining pennies, die, and brass fasteners were remaining after each shake? Why?

3. Determine the half-life of:

   a. The pennies assuming one shake represents 4 years.
   b. The dice assuming one shake represents 15 minutes.
   c. The brass fasteners assuming one shake represents 0.75 seconds.

4. Using the half-lives determined in question #3, calculate:

   a. The age of the penny shoe box when only 10 pennies remain.
   b. The age of the die shoe box when only 50 die remain.
   c. The age of the brass fastener shoe box when only 75 remain.

5. Using the half-lives determined in question #3, what percent of the total number of pennies used in this experiment would be left after 9 years? Percent of die left after 25 minutes? Percent of brass fasteners left after 0.15 seconds?

6. Compare and contrast the usefulness of knowing the half-life of pennies, die, and/or brass fasteners to the usefulness of knowing the half-life of radioactive waste.

Referring to our "Need to Know" board and Nuclear Power Web, where could half-life fit in the problem? How is knowing how to calculate half-life important to nuclear power?

HANDOUT 5.7

DATA TABLES

DATA TABLE A: PENNIES

Total Number of Pennies =					
Shake Number	# of Pennies Removed	# of Pennies Remaining	Shake Number	# of Pennies Removed	# of Pennies Remaining
1			9		
2			10		
3			11		
4			12		
5			13		
6			14		
7			15		
8			16		

DATA TABLE B: DICE

Total Number of Dice =					
Shake Number	# of Dice Removed	# of Dice Remaining	Shake Number	# of Dice Removed	# of Dice Remaining
1			11		
2			12		
3			13		
4			14		
5			15		
6			16		
7			17		
8			18		
9			19		
10			20		

DATA TABLE C: BRASS FASTENERS

Total Number of Brass Fasteners =					
Shake Number	# of Fasteners Removed	# of Fasteners Remaining	Shake Number	# of Fasteners Removed	# of Fasteners Remaining
1			13		
2			14		
3			15		
4			16		
5			17		
6			18		
7			19		
8			20		
9			21		
10			22		
11			23		
12			24		

Handout 5.8

Discussion Questions

Radioisotope	Type of Decay	Half-Life	How long will it take to lose		
			3/4 of its radioactivity	7/8 of its radioactivity	1/10 of its radioactivity
Natural Elements					
Uranium-235	Alpha	7.10×10^8 Yrs.			
Uranium-238	Alpha			1.35×10^{10} Yrs.	
Transuranics					
Plutonium-238	Alpha		172 Yrs.		
Plutonium-239	Alpha	24,400 Yrs.			
Plutonium-240	Alpha			19,740 Yrs.	
Plutonium-241	Beta		26.4 Yrs.		
Americium-241	Alpha	458 Yrs.			
Americium-243	Alpha				1,474 Yrs.
Neptunium-239	Beta		4.7 Yrs.		
Fission Products					
Cerium-144	Beta			2.40 Yrs.	
Cesium-137	Beta		66.4 Yrs.		
Iodine-131	Beta				38.74 Hrs.
Krypton-85	Beta	10.72 Yrs.			
Molybdenum-99	Beta		133.4 Hrs.		
Strontium-90	Beta	28.1 Yrs.			
Xenon-133	Beta		10.54 Days		
Other Radioactive Materials					
Praseodymium-144	Beta	17.3 Mins.			
Barium-137	Alpha		3.04 Mins.		
Thorium-231	Beta				5.1 Hrs.
Thorium-234	Beta		48.2 Days		
Uranium-234	Alpha	247,000 Yrs.			
Americium-241	Alpha			1,374 Yrs.	
Neptunium-237	Alpha				4.28×10^5 Yrs.
Neptunium-239	Beta	2.35 Days			
Technetium-99	Gamma		12 Hrs.		
Yttrium-90	Alpha	64 Hrs.			

DISCUSSION QUESTIONS

1. What is the general relationship between the intensity of radioactivity and half-life? Explain your answer.

2. In your own words, explain the significance of all the above information as it relates to permanently disposing of radioactive waste.

HANDOUT 5.9

DECAY PRODUCTS OF RADIOISOTOPES

Radioisotope	Type of Decay	Half-Life	Radioactive Decay Products		
			Product of Decay	Type of Decay	Half-Life
Natural Elements					
Uranium-235	Alpha	7.10×10^8 Yrs.	Thorium-231	Beta	25.5 Hrs.
Uranium-238	Alpha	4.5×10^9 Yrs.	Thorium-234	Beta	24.1 days
Transuranics					
Plutonium-238	Alpha	86 Yrs.	Uranium-234	Alpha	247,000 Yrs.
Plutonium-239	Alpha	24,400 Yrs.	Uranium-235	Alpha	7.10×10^8 Yrs.
Plutonium-240	Alpha	6,580 Yrs.	Uranium-236	Alpha	2.39×10^7 Yrs.
Plutonium-241	Beta	13.2 Yrs.	Americium-241	Alpha	458 Yrs.
Americium-241	Alpha	458 Yrs.	Neptunium-237	Alpha	2.14×10^6 Yrs.
Americium-243	Alpha	7,370 Yrs.	Neptunium-239	Beta	2.35 Days
Neptunium-239	Beta	2.35 Days	Plutonium-239	Alpha	24,400 Yrs.
Fission Products					
Cerium-144	Beta	285 Days	Praseo-dymium-144	Beta	17.3 Mins.
Cesium-137	Beta	30.2 Yrs.	Barium-137	Alpha	1.52 Mins.
Iodine-131	Beta	8.07 Days	Xenon-131	Stable	
Krypton-85	Beta	10.72 Yrs.	Redidium-85	Stable	
Molybdenum-99	Beta	66.7 Hrs.	Technetrium-99	Gamma	6 Hours
Strontium-90	Beta	28.1 Yrs.	Yttrium-90	Alpha	64 Hours
Xenon-133	Beta	5.27 days	Cesium-133	Stable	

DISCUSSION QUESTIONS

1. Discuss the implications the information contained in the chart on page 135 has on nuclear waste disposal. In particular, the fission products.

2. What do you think is meant by the term "decay chain"?

3. Identify the longest decay chain possible on this handout. Why is it the longest?

HANDOUT 5.10

CHALLENGE QUESTIONS

1. What percentage of the original radioactivity of a quantity of a radioisotope remains after each half-life?

   1   2   3   4   5   6   7   8   9   10

   —   —   —   —   —   —   —   —   —   —

2. Using a piece of graph paper, plot the decay curve from the data in question #1. Try to draw a smooth curved line connecting each point. (Half-life should be on the horizontal axis, while percent should be on the vertical axis.)

3. Using the graph from question #2:

   a. What percent of quantity will be left after 2 1/2 half-lives?

   b. How many half-lives does it take to be left with only 10% of the original radioisotope?

   c. If each half-life represents 75 seconds, how long would it take to reduce the radioactivity of the original radioisotope to 5% of its original value?

4. Radium has a half-life of 1,600 years. Approximately how long does it take for 1% of a sample of radium to decay?

5. Xenon-133 has a half-life of 5.27 days. Approximately low long does it take for 17% of a sample of radium to decay?

6. Scientists believe the earth is 4.6 billion years old. Calculate what percent of the Uranium-238 originally present is here now if the half-life of Uranium-238 is 4.5 billion years?

7. A certain amount of Uranium-235 remains in the fuel rods of a nuclear reactor after it is used to produce power. The left over Uranium-235 is part of the waste that now needs to be disposed of permanently. If originally only one ounce of Uranium-235 is left over, how long would it take for 0.00005 ounces of lead-207 to be produced through the following decay chain?

	Half-Life
U-235	7.10 x 10^8 Years
Th-231	25.5 Hours
Pa-231	27 Days
Ac-227	10 Days
Fr-223	4.8 Minutes
Ra-223	1,600 Years
Rn-219	3.8 Days
Po-215	4.2 x 10^6 Seconds
Pb-211	3.3 Hours
Bi-211	47 Minutes
Tl-207	2.20 Minutes
Pb-207	Stable

Safety Issues Relating to Radiation

LESSON LENGTH: 1 session to introduce, 1 session to complete

INSTRUCTIONAL PURPOSE

- To introduce the safety issue related to nuclear power.

MATERIALS AND HANDOUTS

"Need to Know" board

Nuclear Power Web

Aging nuclear power plants: Managing plant life and decommissioning.

> **Ordering instructions:** Follow the instructions on the order form located at the end of this lesson. This book is necessary for executing lessons #6 and #9 and is a good source of information for other lessons in this unit.

Handout 6.1: "How Safe Is Safe Enough" Discussion Questions

Handout 6.2: Student Brainstorming Worksheet

Handout 6.3: Student Experimental Worksheet

Handout 6.4: Student Protocol Worksheet

Session 1

THINGS TO DO

1. Discuss the "Need to Know" board and Nuclear Power Web in terms of safe operations of the power plant and radiation safety with people.

2. Allow students to read *Box 1-0—"How Safe Is Safe Enough?"* on page 12 of the above book.

3. Break students into small groups and allow them to discuss their thoughts on this excerpt and respond to the questions on Handout 6.1.

4. Bring the students back into the large group. With the remaining session time, conduct a brainstorming activity to allow students to generate topics under nuclear power plant safety. The best option is to produce another web with nuclear power safety at the center.

5. Have students read the following sections from the book before beginning the next session:

   - "Causes and Effects of Nuclear Power Plant Aging," pages 37–44
   - "Safety Practices Addressing Aging," pages 42–52.
   - "Health and Safety Goals for Aging Plants," pages 61–71.

THINGS TO ASK

- What role does safety play in our problem?
- Do you think it is necessary to look at safety before making a decision? Why?
- Could we web our ideas about safety?
- How will this help us conceptualize safety in a nuclear plant?

ASSESSMENT

Participation in webbing and small/large group discussion.

EXTENSIONS

Wolfson, R. (1993). *Nuclear choices: A citizen's guide to nuclear technology.* Cambridge, MA: The MIT Press. (ISBN 0-262-73108-8)

This book is strongly recommended as an additional reading source—not just for this lesson, but for the unit as a whole.

Session 2

THINGS TO DO

1. Now that the students have read the selections, consult the "Need to Know" board and discuss what has changed.

2. Raise questions about the potential biases of what was read, since it was produced by the federal government.

3. Allow the class to point out the *main* areas of interest concerning safety that they need to investigate further.

4. Have students re-read *"Box 2-T—Estimating Health Impacts from Public Radiation Exposure"* from "Safety Practices Addressing Aging" in the previous session and the CAFSE letter from the supplementary information for Lesson 1.

5. Discuss how these positions can be different on the same issue.

6. Break the class into small groups and pass out Handout 6.2, Handout 6.3, and Handout 6.4. Have students design an experiment to test in the following scenario:

    You are a researcher who wants to know if radiation from nuclear power sources (i.e Alpha particles, Beta particles, gamma radiation, etc.) causes cancer in humans. You have no funding or material constraints.

7. Once the groups have had time to do this, bring the class back together and discuss why, ethically, you *cannot* do this type of experimentation on people. Emphasize that since you can't experiment on human subjects, it is virtually impossible to say radiation *causes* cancer.

THINGS TO ASK

- How has the problem changed?
- What do you think about the reading?
- What aspects of safety are the most important? Safety of the citizens? Workers?
- What is the relationship between radiation and cancer? How do we know?
- What is the public opinion on nuclear power and cancer? Health?
- What is the best (or worst) example of safety gone wrong that we can examine for information? How about Chernobyl?

- What is the single largest safety precaution used by power plants to avoid radiating workers, the environment, etc.? (shielding)

ASSESSMENT

Experimental Design Worksheets

EXTENSIONS

1. Looking at other forms of study-designs besides experimentation and what they can tell us (i.e., correlations, observations, epidemiological, etc.).

2. Draw comparisons between cigarette smoking and cancer vs. radiation and cancer.

HANDOUT 6.1

"HOW SAFE IS SAFE ENOUGH" DISCUSSION QUESTIONS

1. Why is "absolute protection," and "total absence of risk," neither a possible nor meaningful goal for nuclear plants? Why can it not be?

2. What other aspects of "everyday life" offer as much, or more, risk to people than a nuclear power plant? Why?

3. What precautions would make *you* feel safe living in a neighborhood with a nuclear power facility? Why?

1. What do we need to find out? (What is the scientific problem?)

2. What materials do we have available?

3. How can we use these materials to help us find out?

4. What do we think will happen? (What is our hypothesis?)

5. What will we need to observe or measure in order to find out the answer to our scientific question?

Adapted from Cothron, J. G., Giese, R. N., & Rezba, R. J. (1989). *Students and research*. Dubuque, IA: Kendall/Hunt Publishing Co.

Title of Experiment:

Hypothesis (Educated guess about what will happen):

Independent Variable (The variable that **you change**):

Dependent Variable (The variable that responds to changes in the independent variable):

Observations/Measurements to Make:

Constants (All the things or factors that remain the same):

Control (The standard for comparing experimental effects):

1. List the materials you will need.

2. Write a step-by-step description of what you will do (like a recipe!). List every action you will take during the experiment.

3. What data will you be collecting?

4. Design a data table to collect and analyze your information.

ORDERING INSTRUCTIONS

1. Photocopy this page and cut along the dotted line.

2. Fill out the order form in full.

3. Mail to the address at the bottom of the form.

4. It would be best to get the material as soon as possible so the flow of the lessons in *Hot Rods* is not interrupted because of unavailable material.

- -

Superintendent of Documents **Publications** Order Form

Order Processing Code:

*7173

P3
Telephone orders (202) 783-3238
To fax your orders (202) 512-2250

☐ **YES**, please send me the following:

Charge your order.
It's Easy!

_____ copies of *Aging Nuclear Power Plants: Managing Plant Life and Decommissioning (192 pages),* S/N 052-003-01342-8 at $11.00 each.

The total cost of my order is $_____. International customers please add 25%. Prices include regular domestic postage and handling and are subject to change.

Please Choose Method of Payment:

_____
(Company or Personal Name)   (Please type or print)

☐ Check Payable to the Superintendent of Documents

_____
(Additional address/attention line)

☐ GPO Deposit Account ☐☐☐☐☐☐☐ — ☐

☐ VISA or MasterCard Account

_____
(Street address)

☐☐☐☐☐☐☐☐☐☐☐☐☐☐☐☐☐☐☐☐☐

_____
(City, State, ZIP Code)

☐☐☐☐ (Credit card expiration date)

Thank you for your order!

_____
(Daytime phone including area code)

_____
(Authorizing Signature)   (9/93)

_____
(Purchase Order No.)

YES NO

May we make your name/address available to other mailers? ☐ ☐

Mail To: New Orders, Superintendent of Documents, P.O. Box 371954, Pittsburgh, PA 15250-7954

THIS FORM MAY BE PHOTOCOPIED

Lesson 7

Background Radiation

LESSON LENGTH: 1 session

INSTRUCTIONAL PURPOSE

- To allow students to directly observe the background radiation in their environment.

MATERIALS AND HANDOUTS

Peanut butter jar

Dark colored fabric (black velveteen is best)

Rubbing alcohol

A block of dry ice large enough to hold the peanut butter jar

Corrugated cardboard

Movie projector or slide projector to provide a beam of light

Plastic tray to hold dry ice

Resource materials on radiation

Amateur Scientist column from *Scientific American*, September, 1952, p. 179.

Handout 7.1: Simple Cloud Chamber

Handout 7.2: Electromagnetic Spectrum

Handout 7.3: Problem Log Questions

Handout 7.4: Problem Log Questions

THINGS TO DO

1. Discuss radiation with students. Ask them whether or not radiation is a naturally occurring phenomenon or one only generated by artificial means. Through the course of the conversation, probe students for their knowledge about background radiation and its effects. Encourage students to consider the difference between background radiation and other forms of radiation. Ask students why information about background radiation might be important while considering the nuclear power plant problem.

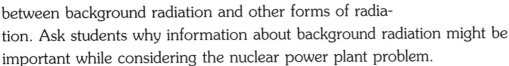

2. Have students consult in-class resources to get answers to some of the basic questions that arise during the discussion.

3. Assemble the cloud chamber as shown in the attached diagram.

4. Block all light from the room. A single projector beam from a movie/slide projector or a strong flashlight should be placed directly to one side of the cloud chamber.

5. Have students watch the chamber and make observations about what they see. Have them discuss the number of times they see a vapor trail inside the cloud chamber. Ask students to speculate about the amount of background radiation they encounter based on this evidence.

6. If background radiation happens to be low (i.e., no visible trails are produced), place a radioactive source such as a 1930's or 40's watch with a radium dial in the chamber and repeat. Please follow safety guidelines for handling radioactive materials. There may be too much shielding in your classroom. Try taking the cloud chamber outside and putting it inside a large dark box.

7. Students should be provided with resource materials so they can find basic information as questions arise.

8. Have students complete Problem Log Questions (Handouts 7.3 and 7.4).

NOTE TO TEACHER

BACKGROUND RADIATION

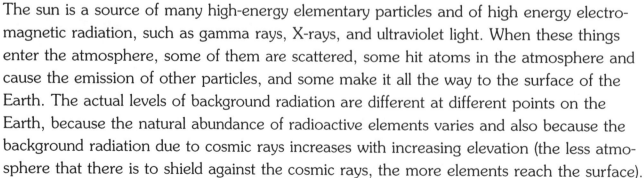

Human beings are constantly exposed to naturally occurring background radiation, and any discussion of the risks associated with human use of radioactive materials must also explore the existence and effects of the radiation that we normally experience. There are two principal natural sources of this background radiation: radioactive decay of elements in our surroundings and cosmic rays that originate in space.

The sun is a source of many high-energy elementary particles and of high energy electromagnetic radiation, such as gamma rays, X-rays, and ultraviolet light. When these things enter the atmosphere, some of them are scattered, some hit atoms in the atmosphere and cause the emission of other particles, and some make it all the way to the surface of the Earth. The actual levels of background radiation are different at different points on the Earth, because the natural abundance of radioactive elements varies and also because the background radiation due to cosmic rays increases with increasing elevation (the less atmosphere that there is to shield against the cosmic rays, the more elements reach the surface).

Resources for basic information about cloud chambers and more complex cloud chambers:

Scientific American
December, 1956, p. 169
April, 1956, p. 156
June, 1959, p. 173

SAFETY GUIDELINES:

Caution: Dry ice must be handled with care.

1. Dry ice must not be tasted, placed near the mouth, or allowed to touch the skin, as the extremely low temperature could cause a burn.

2. Dry ice must not be placed in glass jars or tightly sealed containers. They could explode due to the high pressure.

3. Do not breathe the gas from dry ice for an extended period in a closed area, such as a car. Store the dry ice in a container such as a styrofoam cooler until you are ready to use it.

4. When the dry ice has served its purpose and you no longer have any use for it, open the container and let the dry ice dissipate in a safe place, preferably outside where students or others will not find it and play with it.

THINGS TO ASK

- Is radiation only man-made? What are natural sources of radiation?

- What man-made sources of radiation are in our daily lives?

- Why aren't people concerned about background radiation if radiation is so harmful?

- How could we tell how much radioactive decay is in the room right now?

- If you could see radioactive decay in the room, what would you be interested in knowing?

- What do you see in the cloud chamber?

- What could be producing the radioactive decay in the room?

- Do the particles you see appear to be different from one another in any way? What differences do you see?

- What new perspective does this give you on the issue of radioactive decay which comes from nuclear power plants?
- What additional information do you need about radiation in order to understand the difference (list these on the "Need to Know" board).

ASSESSMENT

Student observations listed in the Problem Log.

EXTENSIONS

1. Radon Gas: Another way that students can explore background radiation is through the use of radon detectors. Radon is a radioactive gas that is produced by the radioactive decay of other elements in rocks or soil. Certain parts of the United States have high concentrations of these elements in their soil; this can result in high concentrations of radon gas in buildings, particularly in areas such as basements. The government has encouraged people to test their homes for radon, as it is thought that long-term exposure to radon can significantly increase a person's risk of lung cancer, particularly if that person also smokes. Radon detectors are relatively cheap and readily available. Students could design a testing protocol for their school and/or their homes.

   Resources for more information:
   Consumer Reports
   October, 1989, p. 623
   July, 1987, p. 440
   January, 1990

2. Find out what research has been done to determine whether travel in an airplane exposes one to more radiation than one would be exposed to on the ground.

HANDOUT 7.1
SIMPLE CLOUD CHAMBER

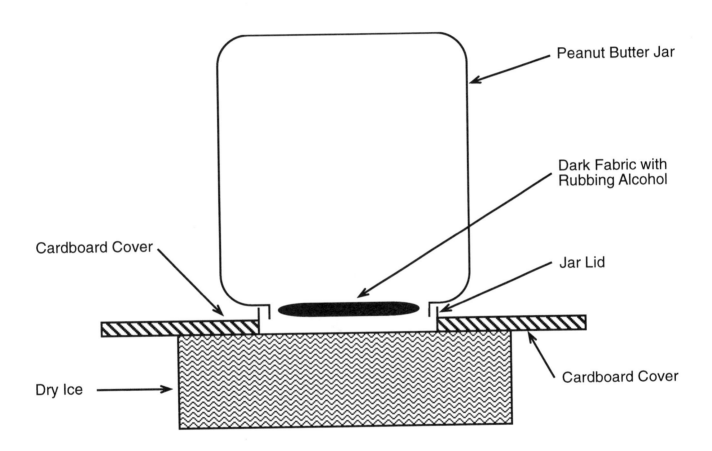

Peanut Butter Jar

Dark Fabric with Rubbing Alcohol

Cardboard Cover

Jar Lid

Dry Ice

Cardboard Cover

Adapted from Amateur Scientist Column. (September, 1952). *Scientific American.* p. 179.

HANDOUT 7.2

ELECTROMAGNETIC SPECTRUM

All of the indicated forms of radiation are identical except for wavelength and frequency.

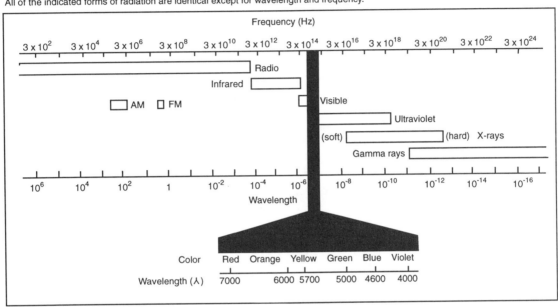

WAVELENGTHS AND FREQUENCIES OF ELECTROMAGNETIC RADIATION

Type of Radiation	Wavelength Range	Frequency Range
Gamma rays	$< 10^{-4}$	$> 3 \times 10^{19}$ Hz
X rays	$1–200 \times 10^{-8}$	$1.5 \times 10^{16}–3 \times 10^{19}$
Extreme ultraviolet	$200–900 \times 10^{-8}$	$3.3 \times 10^{15}–1.5 \times 10^{16}$
Ultraviolet	$900–4000 \times 10^{-8}$	$7.5 \times 10^{14}–3.3 \times 10^{15}$
Visible	$4000–7000 \times 10^{-8}$	$4.3 \times 10^{14}–7.5 \times 10^{14}$
Near infrared	$0.7–20 \times 10^{-4}$	$1.5 \times 10^{13}–4.3 \times 10^{14}$
Far infrared	$20–100 \times 10^{-4}$	$3.0 \times 10^{12}–1.5 \times 10^{13}$
Radio	> 0.01	$< 3 \times 10^{12}$
(Radar)	$(2–20)$	$(1.5–15 \times 10^9)$
(FM radio)	$(250–350)$	$(85–110 \times 10^6)$
(AM radio)	$(18,000–55,000)$	$(550–1600 \times 10^3)$

*All wavelengths are given in centimeters; recall that 1×10^{-8} cm = 1 Angstrom; and 1×10^{-4} cm = 1 micron (10^{-6} meter)

Adapted from *Essentials of the Dynamic Universe, Third Edition* by T. P. Snow; copyright 1970 by West Publishing Company.

Record observations about what you see in the cloud chamber. Observations should include what the output of the cloud chamber looks like; similarities and differences among the different particles observed; estimate of number of particles observed at any given time; and so on.

We've been talking about systems in this unit: the system of generating nuclear power, the system of a nuclear power plant, the system of nuclear power regulation, and so on. Is the cloud chamber a system? Defend your response.

Lesson 8

Shielding Experiment

LESSON LENGTH: 1 session to plan; 1 session to do the experiment & discuss

PURPOSE AND RELATIONSHIP TO OVERALL UNIT GOALS

- To introduce experimental design in a relevant context.

MATERIALS AND HANDOUTS

Source of ultraviolet light (e.g., black light bulb, plant grow-light bulb, or Tensor desk lamp bulb)

Prism

Ultraviolet light detector (e.g., white cotton T-shirt washed in a detergent that contains brightening agents—*All* or *Tide*)

Shielding Materials: cinderblocks, glass, plastic, aluminum foil; anything that can be tested for its ability to block UV or visible light

Plastic UV-protective glasses

Handout 8.1: Student Brainstorming Worksheet

Handout 8.2: Student Experiment Worksheet

Handout 8.3: Student Protocol Worksheet

Handout 8.4: Laboratory Report Form

Handout 8.5: Problem Log Questions

Handout 8.6: Problem Log Questions

Electromagnetic Spectrum: Refer to Handout 7.2, page 157

THINGS TO DO

1. Review the "Need to Know" board and the Nuclear Energy Web and discuss why shielding would be an important concept to understand and explain at the town meeting. Certainly shielding is an important consideration in power plant design as well as in the safe handling of any radioactive substance.

163

2. Talk about ways to test shielding effects on radiation. Discuss ultraviolet light as being a form of electromagnetic radiation. Students can consult the electromagnetic spectrum chart (Handout 7.2).

3. Show students the materials for the lesson. Break students into small groups and ask them to come up with a method for testing the shielding properties of various substances using the materials available. Pass out a copy of the Student Brainstorming Worksheet (Handout 8.1) and have them fill it out.

4. Discuss the brainstorming results as a class.

5. Pass out copies of the Student Experiment Worksheet (Handout 8.2) and have the students complete it.

6. After they have filled out the Student Experiment Worksheet (Handout 8.2), have each group write their protocol on the Student Protocol Worksheet (Handout 8.3). They should include every step they plan to take, the materials they will use, and a data table to record their data. Students should also indicate what safety procedures they plan to use as a part of the overall experimental design.

7. Have students either work individually or in small groups to conduct the experiment. When they have finished, have them complete the Laboratory Report Form (Handout 8.4).

8. After students perform their experiments, bring the group together to discuss their results, limitations of the results, and possible revisions in experimental design. Then have students complete Handouts 8.5 and 8.6.

Safety Precaution: If a commercial research-type UV source is being used, it will be necessary for students to wear plastic UV-protective glasses; long-term exposure to UV can cause cataracts. Also, direct illumination of the skin by the UV source should be avoided; it is possible to be sunburned by these sources.

Sample Protocol

1. In a darkened room, set up a white light source (such as a light bulb), prism, and detector (T-shirt) in such a way that light is spread out by the prism and rainbow falls on the detector (see page 165).

2. Place the shielding material between the prism and the detector. Turn on the lights. Observe the detector.

   - Is any light getting through?

   - Are all colors getting through?

   - Record all observations.

3. Repeat for all available shielding materials.

DATA TABLE

Shielding Material	Description of Material	Description of Spectrum	Shielding Ability

ULTRAVIOLET LIGHT EXPERIMENT DIAGRAM

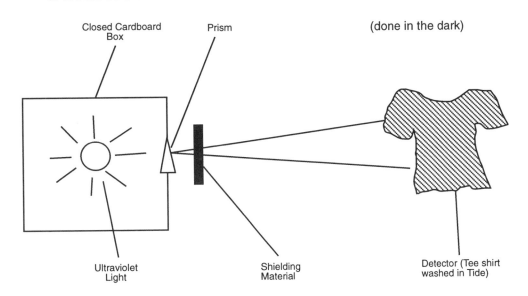

Closed Cardboard Box

Prism

(done in the dark)

Ultraviolet Light

Shielding Material

Detector (Tee shirt washed in Tide)

Observer wearing UV safety glasses.

THINGS TO ASK

- Was there only one way to test the effectiveness of various materials in blocking light?
- How did you know when the light was effectively blocked?
- Did you have any problems with your experiment?
- What might you do differently next time?
- Does this information help to clarify the problem? How?
- What are some problems with this experiment as related to our nuclear energy dilemma?

ASSESSMENT

1. Quality of experimental design developed by students.
2. Evaluation of Laboratory Package.

EXTENSIONS

The results of the experiment will probably raise many more questions about shielding. Some small groups may want to conduct follow-up research doing additional experiments. Students should be encouraged to develop and conduct additional research.

1. What do we need to find out? (What is the scientific problem?)

2. What materials do we have available?

3. How can we use these materials to help us find out?

4. What do we think will happen? (What is our hypothesis?)

5. What will we need to observe or measure in order to find out the answer to our scientific question?

Adapted from Cothron, J. G., Giese, R. N., & Rezba, R. J. (1989). *Students and research.* Dubuque, IA: Kendall/Hunt Publishing Co.

HANDOUT 8.2

STUDENT EXPERIMENT WORKSHEET

Title of Experiment:

Hypothesis (Educated guess about what will happen):

Independent Variable (The variable that **you change**):

Dependent Variable (The variable that responds to changes in the independent variable):

Observations/Measurements to Make:

Constants (All the things or factors that remain the same):

Control (The standard for comparing experimental effects):

1. List the materials you will need.

2. Write a step-by-step description of what you will do (like a recipe!). List every action you will take during the experiment.

3. What data will you be collecting?

4. Design a data table to collect and analyze your information.

HANDOUT 8.4

LABORATORY REPORT FORM

1. What did you do or test? (Include your experiment title.)

2. How did you do it? Cite materials and methods. You can go back to your Student Protocol Worksheet (Handout 8.3) and use the information from the first two questions.

3. What did you find out? (Include a data summary and the explanation of its meaning.)

4. What did you learn from your experiment?

5. What further questions do you now have?

6. Does the information you learned help with the problem?

1. Does shielding bear any importance to the topic you are investigating? If so, what is its significance? If not, why not?

2. Does this new information make the problem look different than it did previously? If so, restate the problem based on the new information; if not, state why the problem can remain as stated.

PROBLEM LOG QUESTIONS

Is there such a thing as a 100% effective shield? At what point is there too much radiation? What's the best material available now for radiation protection?

A Look at Chernobyl

LESSON LENGTH: Variable, with a minimum of 1 session

INSTRUCTIONAL PURPOSE

- To allow students to investigate the "worst case scenario" in terms of safety, biological effects of radiation, and long term radiation effects.
- To help students understand possible risks by looking at past events.

MATERIALS AND HANDOUTS

Shcherbak, Y.M. (1996). Ten years of the Chernobyl era. *Scientific American*, April, 44-49.

Edwards, M. (1994). Living with a monster: Chernobyl. *National Geographic, 186* (2), 100-115.

Handout 9.1: Problem Log Questions

THINGS TO DO

1. Have students read the articles above and write down notes about their thoughts and feelings.

2. In a large group setting, conduct an open discussion on what they read. If possible, arrange the classroom into a circle for the discussion.

3. Allow students to explore the Chernobyl accident. Interject only when they are going too far from the topic. This creates an atmosphere of free discussion.

4. Direct the discussion toward similarities/differences of Chernobyl and the Maple Island plant.

5. Close by having students respond to the Problem Log Questions (Handout 9.1).

THINGS TO ASK

- Please share your thoughts and feelings on what you have read.

- How is the Chernobyl incident related to our problem?

- Could the Chernobyl accident have been prevented with better safety precautions?

- Have the long-term health effects of the Chernobyl accident been consistent with what we know of the biological effects of radiation?

- What can we learn from Chernobyl that will improve the safety of Riverton?

ASSESSMENT

Evaluation of student responses during the free-discussion problem log.

EXTENSIONS

1. It would be appropriate to allow more student investigations into Chernobyl if there is interest.

2. Compare/contrast the Chernobyl accident and the 3-Mile Island accident.

The following video is strongly recommended for viewing if it can be obtained. At present it is no longer in production, but existing copies can be obtained. It gives a firsthand look at the Chernobyl accident.

Chernobyl: A chronicle of difficult weeks. Glasnost Film Festival, Vol. #4. This is a Russian documentary film with English subtitles. Released in the U.S. by:

The Video Project
5332 College Ave., Suite 101
Oakland, CA 94618
1-800-4-PLANET

PROBLEM LOG QUESTIONS

1. Taking into account all that has been covered thus far, including what you know about the Chernobyl accident, how has the problem evolved? Is it the same as when you started? Has the mayor's responsibility grown?

2. With all the safety precautions we have looked at, could a disaster like Chernobyl happen at the Maple Island Nuclear Power Plant? What steps could be taken to reduce the risk? Explain.

lesson

10

Consultation with an Expert

LESSON LENGTH: 3 sessions

INSTRUCTIONAL PURPOSE

- To provide interaction with a professional working in a radiation related field. *(Suggestions for a speaker: a medical doctor, a power plant representative, a nuclear researcher, a radiation safety officer, a representative from the Nuclear Regulatory Commission.)*

MATERIALS AND HANDOUTS

Chart and markers

Audio-Visual equipment for guest speaker

Handout 10.1: Visitor Planning Sheet

Session 1
Before the Speaker Comes

THINGS TO DO

1. Brainstorm with students, deciding what questions need to be asked of the speaker. Use the "Need to Know" board to choose questions.

2. Class discussion can help sort questions into most and least important questions.

3. Students should also be guided to think about the best way to phrase the questions. Are they specific enough? Are they too specific?

4. Group questions can be recorded on a master question chart.

5. Students can then add any of their own questions to individual Visitor Planning Sheets (Handout 10.1).

183

THINGS TO ASK

- What information do we want to know?
- What information will the guest speaker be most qualified to give?
- What do we want to know by the time the guest speaker leaves?
- What facts do we want to get from this person?
- What opinions would be interesting to have?
- Which of these questions are most important?
- How can we get an idea of this person's perspective on this kind of situation?
- Do you think this person will have a bias? What would it be? How can we find out?

Session 2
The Guest Speaker's Presentation

THINGS TO DO

1. Guest Speaker: The guest provides his/her information regarding the area of his/her expertise.
2. Students take notes and ask their questions.
3. Students should also be prepared to share with the guest speaker background on the problem and their decisions to date.

Session 3
Debriefing

THINGS TO DO

1. In a follow-up to the guest speaker, teacher and students should review the "Need to Know" board, removing questions which have been answered and adding new issues, if necessary.

2. Teachers and students should discuss the potential bias in the information provided by the guest speaker and the possible effects of that bias on the validity of the information.

THINGS TO ASK

- What were the things we learned from the guest speaker?

- How does the new information affect our thinking about the problem?

- Do we need to reorganize our approach to the problem?

- Did this person reveal a particular bias? If so, what?

- Where can we go to get another perspective? A balanced report of information?

ASSESSMENT

1. Students should report in their problem logs information provided by the guest lecturer and reflect on the potential of bias in the Problem Log.

2. Students write a thank-you letter to the guest speaker, detailing which information was particularly helpful.

NOTE TO TEACHER

If the expert comes to the classroom, all students can participate. This format can also be used by small groups who need to interview an outside expert outside of class; afterwards, they can report any new information to the class.

Prior to the visitor coming to make the presentation, it would be helpful to inform him/her of the "problem" and some possible questions the students might have.

HANDOUT **10.1**

VISITOR PLANNING SHEET

Student Name _____

Name of Visitor _____

Who is this visitor?

_____

_____

_____

Why is this visitor coming to see us?

_____

_____

Why is this visitor important to us?

_____

_____

_____

What would you like to tell our visitor about our problem?

_____

_____

What questions do you want to ask the visitor?

_____

_____

_____

Lesson 11

Waste Management: Research on Options

LESSON LENGTH: 1 planning session; several research sessions

INSTRUCTIONAL PURPOSE

- To help students research and synthesize information in order to both understand a particular aspect of nuclear waste management and teach it to others.

MATERIALS AND HANDOUTS

Handout 11.1: Group Investigation Guidelines
Handout 11.2: Group Investigation Plan of Action
Handout 11.3: Group Investigation: Teacher Evaluation
Handout 11.4: Memorandum to the Mayor

THINGS TO DO

1. Discuss the "Need to Know" board and Nuclear Power Web in terms of waste management, focusing on the problem.

2. Provide students with a copy of the Group Investigation Guidelines (Handout 11.1) which should be discussed to clarify expectations for their discussion at the town meeting.

3. Present to the class Handout 11.4 which should set up the four topics to be researched by the groups. Once the students have read the handout, have the class split into four groups. Each group will research one of the areas on the handout: on-site (storage pools or above ground), transport to (permanent repository or M.R.S.).

4. Have students convene in small groups to plan how they will investigate their topics (use Handout 11.2 as a guide). Students should be encouraged to web their group topics just as they did the problem. Students should be encouraged to com-

pare the individual webs they completed in their Problem Logs. Webs representing a consensus among group members can be created.

5. Students should create a list of questions about their topics and think about available resources for obtaining the necessary information.

6. During subsequent sessions, groups should meet to share and synthesize information, planning how to present the information to the class. At this point, students should receive a copy of the evaluation form (Handout 11.3) that provides the criteria on which the student will be evaluated. The teacher may wish to modify this form to reflect school practices. Teacher and students should address during large group sessions which information is best instructed to small groups and which information should be presented to the class as a whole.

THINGS TO ASK

- What information will you need to present to the town about your topic to help people understand nuclear power? Why do they need to know this?

- What will be the best sources of information for you to use to fully investigate your topic?

- What will be the best way for you to present this information to the town?

- Do the townspeople need to understand any other topic in order to understand yours?

- How does your information relate to the overall nuclear energy web we created?

- What if the needed information is specific to a particular group? Is there any information here which everyone needs to understand?

- What's the most efficient way of getting some of this information?

ASSESSMENT

Group Investigation Plan of Action.

EXTENSIONS

Other areas may be investigated by students. The following topics were investigated by students in the pilot test classes.

    A. Nuclear Power Plant Design

    B. Alternative Energy Sources

C. Government Agencies Associated with Nuclear Power

D. Accidents at Nuclear Power Plants

E. Effects of Radiation on Humans and Ecosystems

F. Conventional Uses of Nuclear Power

G. Radioactive Waste

H. Advantages and Disadvantages of Nuclear Power

NOTE TO TEACHER

As students investigate their nuclear energy topics and prepare for
the upcoming town council meeting, they should encounter a good
deal of information about nuclear energy. Students should be encouraged to gather information from a variety of sources, including
print material, guest speakers, telephone interviews with local officials,
and computer data bases. As a general rule, the more information
students get from outside sources or on their own, the better. However, if
the entire class seems to need a particular body of information, the teacher may want to
have a "Time Out" session where some basic information is presented through a lecture,
science demonstration, or form`flÄexperiment. Specific large-group lessons or activities
should help support the topics that students are investigating and should be designed to
answer "Need to Know" questions.

The Harvard *Project Physics* (1975) or *PSSC* (Haber-Schaim, Dodge, & Walter, 1986)
materials both provide much background information and interesting activities to support
this content outline. Teachers should adapt activities either for small groups or for the entire
class in order to respond to the "Need to Know" questions. Field trip(s) and guest speakers
provide important opportunities for students to get answers to their questions.

Following are a list of excellent references relating to nuclear physics, nuclear power, and/
or nuclear waste management:

Haber-Schaim, V., Dodge, J.H. & Walter, J.A. (1986). *PSSC Physics*. Lexington, MA: D.C.
Heath & Co.

Meller, P. (1991). Our electric future: A comeback for nuclear power? *National Geographic,
180* (2), 60-89.

OCRUM (1990). *Science, secrecy, and America's nuclear waste: The waste management
system.* Washington, DC: U.S. Department of Energy.

OCRUM Information Center
Attn: Curriculum Department
P.O. Box 44375
Washington, DC 20020
(800) 225-6972

Project Physics. (1975). NY: Holt, Rinehart & Winston, Inc.

Windows on Science. (1990). Warren, NJ: Optical Data Corporation.

Whipple, C.G. (1996). Can nuclear waste be stored safely at Yucca Mountain? *Scientific American*, June, 72-79.

HANDOUT 11.1

GROUP INVESTIGATION GUIDELINES

Step 1: Choose a topic.

Step 2: WEBBING: Brainstorm information concerning the chosen topic. Include related problems which might exist. Consider "not-so-obvious" problems, consider problems related to:

- Economy
- Politics and Diplomacy
- Sociology
- News Media
- Volunteer Work
- Education
- Religion
- Transportation
- Health and Medicine

Step 3: Develop questions you would like to have answered about the topic and tell where you would go to find the answers.

Step 4: Write a HYPOTHESIS about the topic to be investigated.

Step 5: Develop a PLAN OF ACTION to develop/test the Thesis Statement:

- Outline procedures or sequential plan of action
- Decide on deadline for the study
- Consider audience
- Consider method of presentation: written, oral, display, model, multi-media, other

Step 6: Implement the PLAN OF ACTION:

- Review the literature
- Collect data and record information
- Record bibliographic information
- Analyze data

Step 7: DRAW CONCLUSIONS. Examine the identified problem to see if questions have been answered. Make recommendations for further research.

Step 8: Develop a bibliography of sources throughout the research.

Step 9: Presentation of Results: Timeline, Poster/Charts, Oral Presentations, Mural, Diorama, etc.

Group Investigation Plan of Action

Name of Topic:

Topic Web of Information Needed to Understand Topic:

Specific Questions That Need to be Researched:

Possible Sources of Information:

Who Will Do What When?

How Will You Present Your Information at the Town Meeting?

HANDOUT 11.3

GROUP INVESTIGATION: TEACHER EVALUATION

Name: _____

Topic: _____

Date: _____

EVALUATION CRITERIA

Topic/Problem _____

- Is the topic meaningful and interesting to the student?
- Is the topic "reality based"?
- Does the thesis statement provide a focus for the investigation?

Data Collection _____

- Is the webbing comprehensive?
- Does the web reveal the "whole picture" concerning the general topic?
- Are the questions generated meaningfully, appropriately, and are they well written?
- Are the sources selected appropriate for the topic?
- Was a variety of primary and secondary sources selected?
- Is the bibliography correctly written?

Data Organization _____

- Was the data organized effectively in order to facilitate communication and understanding?
- Were visual aids relevant to the investigation?
- Does the conclusion synthesize the research?

Presentation of Data _____

- Was the presentation interesting and effective?
- Did the presenter follow the forensics guidelines discussed in class?
- Did the presenter interact with the audience effectively?

Other Considerations _____

- Time on Task
- Student growth throughout the investigation process
- Does the investigation reflect "true research"?

Overall Performance _____

Comments: _____

_____

_____

_____

_____

_____

_____

_____

ACME Power

"Pioneers in the Power Industry"
Department of Waste Management

Memorandum

To: Mayor Christine Barrett's office

From: Jerry Brown, Vice President of Waste Management

Date:

Re: Expansion of Waste Facilities

Much discussion has risen over the planned expansion of the waste disposal pools. I realize much of the decision rests on your shoulders, and I feel it is my responsibility as Vice President of Waste Management and as your friend to inform you of alternatives to expanding the waste pools.

Expanding the waste pools is just one method of on-site disposal, but others do exist. Another possibility is an above-ground storage facility made of concrete, steel, etc. Presently, the Surry Nuclear Power Facility in Surry, VA practices this technique safely and successfully.

In addition to on-site disposal, we could transport our nuclear waste to other sites across the U.S. Obviously, more approvals at those sites will have to be made before any implementation. The Department of Energy is working on a permanent repository at Yucca Mountain, NV and Monitored Retrievable Storage (M.R.S.) facilities across the U.S. to handle the problems of storing the growing amount of the nation's nuclear waste.

I hope this information helps you work toward a good decision for all involved.

Lesson 12

On-Site Storage

LESSON LENGTH: 1 session

INSTRUCTIONAL PURPOSE

- To provide an opportunity for students to add additional information to problem by oral presentation to the class.

MATERIALS AND HANDOUTS

Handout 12.1: Oral Presentation Critique

Handout 12.2: Self-Evaluation

THINGS TO DO

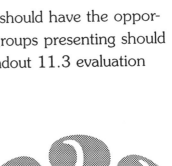

1. Have each of the two groups researching on-site disposal methods (i.e., storage pools and above ground storage facilities). Present a 15 minute presentation to the class on findings.

2. Once this information has been presented, refer to the "Need to Know" board and Nuclear Power Web for any changes stemming from this new information.

3. Pass out the evaluation sheets to the students. All students should have the opportunity to fill out Handout 12.1 while each member of the groups presenting should also fill out Handout 12.2. Teachers need to complete Handout 11.3 evaluation form.

THINGS TO ASK

- How does this new information fit into our problem?
- Has the problem changed?
- What is the most important aspect of each presentation to consider in our problem?

ASSESSMENT

1. Student Oral Presentation Critiques.
2. Teacher Oral Presentation Critiques.
3. Self-Evaluation.

HANDOUT 12.1

ORAL PRESENTATION CRITIQUE

PEER EVALUATION

Name: _____

Topic: _____

Date: _____

Grade	0	1	2	3
1. Presentation of Ideas	0	1	2	3
2. Clarity of Presentation	0	1	2	3
3. Use of Visual Aids	0	1	2	3
4. Interaction with the Group	0	1	2	3

TOTAL _____

Questions: _____

_____

_____

_____

Constructive Criticism: _____

_____

_____

_____

_____

Rating Scale:
0 = No points: Not Satisfactory
1 = One Point: Satisfactory
2 = Two Points: Extra Effort
3 = Three Points: Outstanding Effort

1. What did you like best about the investigation?

_____

_____

_____

2. What were the most interesting things you learned?

_____

_____

_____

3. Did you give your best effort to the investigation? Explain.

_____

_____

_____

4. How would you rate your overall performance? Explain.

_____

_____

_____

5. Did you use your time wisely throughout the investigation? Explain.

_____

_____

_____

Transport to Repository

LESSON LENGTH: 1 session

INSTRUCTIONAL PURPOSE

- To provide an opportunity for students to add additional information to problem by oral presentation to the class.

MATERIALS AND HANDOUTS

Handout 13.1: Oral Presentation Critique
Handout 13.2: Self-Evaluation

THINGS TO DO

1. Have each of the two groups researching on-site disposal methods (i.e., permanent repository and M.R.S.). Present a 15 minute presentation to the class on findings.

2. Once this information has been presented, refer to the "Need to Know" board and Nuclear Power Web for any changes stemming from this new information.

3. Pass out the evaluation sheets to the students. All students should have the opportunity to fill out Handout 13.1 while each member of the groups presenting should also fill out Handout 13.2. Teachers should complete Handout 11.3 evaluation form.

THINGS TO ASK

- How does this new information fit into our problem?

- Has the problem changed?

- What is the most important aspect of each presentation to consider in our problem?

ASSESSMENT

1. Student Oral Presentation Critiques.

2. Teacher Oral Presentation Critiques.

3. Self-Evaluation.

HANDOUT 13.1

ORAL PRESENTATION CRITIQUE

PEER EVALUATION

Name: _____

Topic: _____

Date: _____

Grade	0	1	2	3
1. Presentation of Ideas	0	1	2	3
2. Clarity of Presentation	0	1	2	3
3. Use of Visual Aids	0	1	2	3
4. Interaction with the Group	0	1	2	3

TOTAL _____

Questions: _____

_____

_____

_____

Constructive Criticism: _____

_____

_____

_____

_____

Rating Scale:
0 = No points: Not Satisfactory
1 = One Point: Satisfactory
2 = Two Points: Extra Effort
3 = Three Points: Outstanding Effort

1. What did you like best about the investigation?

_____

_____

_____

2. What were the most interesting things you learned?

_____

_____

_____

3. Did you give your best effort to the investigation? Explain.

_____

_____

_____

4. How would you rate your overall performance? Explain.

_____

_____

_____

5. Did you use your time wisely throughout the investigation? Explain.

_____

_____

_____

Problem Resolution: Debate and Consensus

LESSON LENGTH: 4 sessions

INSTRUCTIONAL PURPOSE

- To use debate skills to come to problem resolution.

MATERIALS AND HANDOUTS USED

Handout 14.1: Debate Format
Handout 14.2: Persuasive Speech Evaluation Form
Handout 14.3: Reasoning Assessment

Session 1

THINGS TO DO

1. Hand out the worksheet on Debate Format (Handout 14.1) and use it to teach the skill of debating to students.

2. Students in Session 2 will debate the following issue:

   Resolved: That the Maple Island Nuclear Power Plant should be allowed to expand its on-site waste storage facilities.

3. If you want students to have practice in the debate format, have them use an issue such as the following:

   Resolved: Students in our school should be required to wear uniforms.

4. Assign the teams to be for or against the resolution. Allow students time to plan their arguments.

5. Using the procedure outlined in Handout 14.1 have the teams debate. One team debates and the other team scores and marks the argumentative points made. Reverse the roles. (Teachers may want to refer to the following article for more information on debate: Swicord, B. (1984, Summer). Debating with gifted fifth and

sixth graders—Telling it like it was, is, and could be. *Gifted Child Quarterly, 28* (3), pp. 127–129.)

6. Discuss the debate, using the Persuasive Speech Evaluation Form (Handout 14.2) and Reasoning Assessment (Handout 14.3).

7. Refer to the "Need to Know" board and add or change information.

8. If time permits, have students begin preparation for the problem resolution debate. Most of the information needed for the debate should have already been covered in previous lessons.

THINGS TO ASK

- What is the difference between a debate and a discussion?

- What is the traditional set speaking order for a debate?

- How do you prepare for a debate?

- How are debates judged?

Session 2

THINGS TO DO

1. Students will prepare for a debate on the issue:

   Resolved: That the Maple Island Nuclear Power Plant should be allowed to expand its on-site waste storage facilities.

2. Allow one 50-minute session to prepare for the debate.

THINGS TO ASK

- What parts of the "Need to Know" board help us support our topic?

- If more information is needed, where can we get it?

- What counterparts will the other team offer?

Session 3

THINGS TO DO

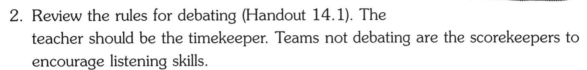

1. Begin the class with two teams debating the issue that was assigned in Session 2:

   Resolved: That the Maple Island Nuclear Power Plant should be allowed to expand its on-site waste storage facilities.

2. Review the rules for debating (Handout 14.1). The teacher should be the timekeeper. Teams not debating are the scorekeepers to encourage listening skills.

3. At the end of fifteen minutes, switch team positions.

4. Score and discuss the debates.

5. Try to come to some class consensus on the problem. What is the stance going to be of the mayor?

THINGS TO ASK

- What is the viewpoint of each side?
- What position are we going to take as mayor? Why?
- What opposes our position?

EXTENSIONS

Students can choose another related topic to research and debate if indecisions arise (such as, worker compensation, role of federal government in making decision, etc.).

Session 4

THINGS TO DO

1. Have students work in their small groups to discuss the merits of both sides of the question of whether Maple Island should be allowed to expand its on-site storage facilities. Each group should take a point of view and should write a statement for the Mayor to present at the Town Meeting. The statement should include supporting reasons.

2. Have each group present its recommendation to the class. Discuss the recommendations and either select one (possibly with minor revisions), combine elements of several, or devise a new solution to be presented to the Town Council.

3. Invite a panel of interested professionals and/or parents to play the Town Council. Hold the Town Council meeting and have the Mayor present the recommendation. Other students should represent various points of view of community members. Students should be prepared to answer questions from the Town Council.

ASSESSMENT

1. Small group recommendations about problem resolution.
2. Participation in Town Council.

WHAT IS A DEBATE?

A series of formal spoken arguments for and against a definite proposal. The best solution is approved and adopted.

Debate is a special type of argument in which two or more speakers present opposing propositions in an attempt to win the audience to their sides. The teams are not concerned with convincing each other. The purpose is to try to alter the audience thinking by presenting the issues honestly with reliable evidence.

WHY DEBATE?

Debate helps you:

1. To analyze problems.

2. Reinforce statements with proof.

3. Express your ideas clearly.

4. Gain confidence.

5. Think quickly.

6. Gain a clear understanding of alternate viewpoints upon reflection.

WHAT ARE THE RULES OF DEBATING?

Debates begin with a proposed solution to a problem. The proposal should begin with the word RESOLVED. Examples:

- Resolved that the United States should abolish the electoral college and elect the President by popular vote.

- Resolved that television has beneficial effects on listeners.

  1. The same number of persons speak on each opposing side.

  2. Begin with careful analysis by both teams on the subject to be debated. Each member should know as much about the opponent's arguments as he does his own position.

3. Decide which arguments are closely related and worthy of being included and which are irrelevant and should be excluded.

4. Chief points of differences between the affirmative and negative sides are the main issues.

5. List the main issues for each side.

6. Find evidence that will prove the issue true and false. (Facts, examples, statistics, testimony)

7. Be prepared to answer the arguments of the other team's issues, called a REBUTTAL.

WHAT IS THE FORMAT FOR A DEBATE?

Suggested Procedure:

> First Affirmative—Affirmative speech—5 minutes
>
> First Negative—Rebuttal—2 minutes
>
> Second Negative—Negative speech—5 minutes
>
> Second Affirmative—Rebuttal—2 minutes

The debate always begins and ends with the affirmative team.
Scoring will be done by giving:

1. One point for an argument and

2. Two points for an argument with proof.

HANDOUT 14.2

PERSUASIVE SPEECH EVALUATION FORM

Name _____

Exercise _____

Directions: Use the following rating scale to evaluate each quality:

   3 = Excellent   2 = Satisfactory   1 = Needs Improvement

	Needs Improvement	Satisfactory	Excellent
The purpose of the speech was clear.	1	2	3
The speaker's reasoning was clear and logical.	1	2	3
The basic components of the argument were evident.	1	2	3
The speaker showed knowledge of the subject.	1	2	3
The speaker addressed opposing points of view.	1	2	3
The speaker was audible, maintained eye contact and spoke with expression.	1	2	3
The speaker held the interest of the audience.	1	2	3

The Best Part of This Speech Was:

_____

_____

A Suggestion for Improvement Is:

_____

_____

HANDOUT 14.3

TEACHER REASONING ASSESSMENT

Name: _____

Date: _____

Directions: Please rate each student on his/her reasoning skills evidenced in oral and written communication.

3 = To a Great Extent	2 = To Some Extent	1 = Not At All

	Not at All	To Some Extent	To a Great Extent
1. To what extent is the reasoning clear?	1	2	3
2. To what extent is the reasoning specific as in citing appropriate examples or illustrations?	1	2	3
3. To what extent is the reasoning logically consistent?	1	2	3
4. To what extent is the reasoning accurate?	1	2	3
5. To what extent is the reasoning complete?	1	2	3

Particular Strengths:

_____

_____

Areas Needing Improvement:

_____

_____

lesson

Final Overall Unit Assessment Activity

INSTRUCTIONAL PURPOSE

- To assess understanding of the scientific content taught by this unit.
- To assess the ability of the student to use appropriate scientific process skills in the resolution of a real-world problem.
- To assess student understanding of the concept of systems.

ESTIMATED TIME

The content assessment should take the students approximately thirty minutes; the experimental design assessment should take the students approximately thirty minutes; and the systems assessment should take the students approximately thirty minutes.

TAILORING THE ASSESSMENTS TO REFLECT STUDENT EXPERIENCES

The list of substances in part C of the content assessment may differ from the list of substances that your students tested in lab. Be sure that it is changed to include ten substances that your students tested.

MATERIALS AND HANDOUTS

Handout 15.1: Final Content Assessment

Handout 15.2: Experimental Design Assessment

Handout 15.3: Systems Assessment

Scoring protocols for Final Content Assessment, Experimental Design Assessment, and Systems Assessment

PROCEDURE

Have students complete assessments found in Handouts 15.1, 15.2, and 15.3.

HANDOUT 15.1

FINAL CONTENT ASSESSMENT (30 MINUTES)

1. Consider the following nuclear reactions:

   a. $_{92}U^{235} + _{0}n^{1} \longrightarrow _{38}Sr^{90} + _{54}Xe^{143} + 3\ _{0}n^{1}$

   b. $_{92}U^{238} \longrightarrow _{90}Th^{234} + _{2}He^{4}$

   Which reaction has the potential to become a chain reaction? Explain your answer.

2. Nuclear power reactors and atomic bombs both get their energy from nuclear reactions, yet nuclear power plants can't produce nuclear explosions, while atomic bombs do. What is a design feature of nuclear power plants that helps to keep them from acting like atomic bombs? How does this design feature work?

3. $_{53}I^{125}$ has a half-life of 60 days. Suppose a scientist has a sample containing 1 millicurie of $_{53}I^{125}$ today. How much $_{53}I^{125}$ will remain in her sample 120 days from now?

4. Everyone is exposed to radiation during their lives. List two sources of everyday radiation exposure.

   a.

   b.

5. Unnecessary radiation exposure can be dangerous. List two health problems that radiation can cause.

   a.

   b.

6. Give an example of a piece of equipment or protective method that can protect a person against unnecessary radiation exposure, and briefly explain how it works to protect people.

You are a biologist, working in a university medical research laboratory that uses small amounts of $_{15}P^{32}$, a radioactive isotope of phosphorous that has a 14 day half-life and is easily shielded with plexiglass. The experiments that you do result in the production of low-level liquid radioactive waste. The liquid waste is stored for later removal in plastic gallon jugs. There is a liquid waste bottle which is kept behind a plexiglass shield on the floor next to your lab bench. For the sake of convenience and to prevent spills, there is a funnel in the neck of the waste bottle; this allows you to safely pour your radioactively contaminated liquids into the jug. The waste bottle is not usually capped; you believe that this is safe, because the radioactive materials that you are using are not volatile (in other words, they won't leave the bottle and contaminate the air.)

Late one night, as you are finishing a long experiment, you notice something disconcerting: a large, brown cockroach has crawled out of the liquid waste bottle and is teetering on the top edge of the funnel. Quickly, you trap the roach in a jar. You take the roach down the hall to the scintillation counter, a machine which will allow you to determine whether the roach contains $_{15}P^{32}$, and, if so, how much. Scintillation counting reveals that the roach (who had to be sacrificed for the sake of the experiment) was, indeed, contaminated with high levels of $_{15}P^{32}$.

You had known that the building was roach-infested, but the possibility that the roaches would drink your radioactive liquid waste had not occurred to you before. You begin to wonder how many other cockroaches have visited your waste bottle. Describe an experiment which will allow you to decide whether radioactive cockroaches pose a contamination problem in your building.

In your answer, include the following:
a. Your hypothesis:

b. The materials you would need:

c. The protocol you would use:

d. A data table showing what data you would collect:

e. A description of how you would use your data to decide whether radioactive roaches did indeed pose a contamination problem for the lab building:

A storage facility for spent nuclear reactor fuel can be thought of as a system.

1. List the parts of the system. Include boundaries, elements, input, and output.

   Boundaries (describe):

   Elements (list at least five):

   Input (list at least two kinds):

   Output (list at least two kinds):

2. Draw a diagram of the system that shows where each of the parts can be found.

3. On your diagram in #2, draw lines (in a different color) showing three important interactions between different parts of the system. Why is each of these interactions important to the system? Explain your answer.

   a. Interaction #1:

   b. Interaction #2:

   c. Interaction #3:

SCORING PROTOCOL

FINAL CONTENT ASSESSMENT

1. **(10 points)** Consider the following nuclear reactions:

    a. $_{92}U^{235} + {}_0n^1 \longrightarrow {}_{38}Sr^{90} + {}_{54}Xe^{143} + 3\,{}_0n^1$

    b. $_{92}U^{238} \longrightarrow {}_{90}Th^{234} + {}_2He^4$

    Which reaction has the potential to become a chain reaction? Explain your answer.

    Only reaction "a" has the potential to become a chain reaction. Reaction "a" uses one neutron and produces three. If conditions are right, these three neutrons can interact with three other atoms of $_{92}U^{235}$ and cause them to fission, producing nine more neutrons, which can then go on to cause even more fission events . . . A reaction whose products have the potential to cause more reactions like it is called a chain reaction.

    Give 5 points for the right answer and 5 points for the right explanation.

2. **(10 points)** Nuclear power reactors and atomic bombs both get their energy from nuclear reactions, yet nuclear power plants can't produce nuclear explosions, while atomic bombs do. What is a design feature of nuclear power plants that helps to keep them from acting like atomic bombs? How does this design feature work?

    Examples include:

    Fuel rod design: keeps the reaction from proceeding too quickly by keeping the fissile atoms (material that is capable of undergoing fission) well-enough separated from each other.

    Presence of a moderator: moderators are substances that absorb neutrons to slow the progress of the chain reaction; control rods are made of such substances.

    Note: *The containment building is not an acceptable answer to this question. While it is a safety device, it has nothing to do with the chain reactions occurring inside.*

    Give 5 points for the design feature and 5 points for the explanation.

3. **(5 points)** $_{53}I^{125}$ has a half-life of 60 days. Suppose a scientist has a vial containing 1 millicurie of $_{53}I^{125}$ today. How much $_{53}I^{125}$ will remain in her vial 120 days from now?

    120 days is two half-lives: thus one-quarter, or 0.25 mCi, of $_{53}I^{125}$ will remain in her vial.

    Give 5 points for the correct answer.

4. **(10 points)** Everyone is exposed to radiation during their lives. List two sources of everyday radiation exposure.

The sun (ultraviolet rays and cosmic rays); radioactive elements naturally present in the world around us (in soil, water, air, and our own bodies); medical treatments (X-rays and radiation therapy, for example).

Give 5 points for each correct answer.

5. **(10 points)** Unnecessary radiation exposure can be dangerous. List two kinds of health problems that radiation can cause.

Cancer, cataracts, genetic defects, radiation burns, sunburn.

Give 5 points for each correct answer.

6. **(5 points)** Give an example of a piece of equipment or protective method that can protect a person against unnecessary radiation exposure, and briefly explain how it works to protect people.

Sunscreen; lead aprons at the dentist's, water in a nuclear fuel rod storage pool: all act as shielding materials because they absorb various kinds of radiation.

Geiger counters and film badges: these items act as detection devices which allow a person to determine whether they are being exposed to dangerous radiation levels.

Give 2.5 points for a correct item and 2.5 points for a correct explanation.

Total number of points possible: 50

SCORING PROTOCOL
EXPERIMENTAL DESIGN ASSESSMENT

. . . Describe an experiment which will allow you to decide whether radioactive cockroaches pose a contamination problem in your building. In your answer, include the following:

    a. **(5 points)** Your hypothesis:

You have already found one highly radioactive roach. If other roaches had also been drinking out of the radioactive waste bottle, they would be radioactive too. Because the waste bottle was open and available to roaches, and because the building is roach-infested, I hypothesize that many other roaches in the building will prove to be highly radioactive, which will indeed be a contamination problem.

Note: *Other hypotheses are possible; accept all reasonable answers; give five points for any reasonable hypothesis.*

    b. **(10 points)** The materials you would need, including any necessary safety equipment:

Scintillation counter and related analyzing equipment
Roach motels
Jars to keep the roaches in, once captured
Jugs for liquid radioactive waste
Waste cans for solid radioactive waste
Plexiglass shielding

Note: *The student only needs to list the detector for radioactive material (3 points), plexiglass shielding to protect herself against possible radiation exposure from the roaches (4 points), and the roaches themselves (3 points): this materials list does not need to be comprehensive.*

Note: *Accept all reasonable materials lists, as long as they're consonant with the hypothesis in part a.*

    c. **(10 points)** The protocol you would use:

As a single, captured, radioactive roach by itself does not constitute a problem, I would need to capture a large number of roaches in the building and check each of them in the scintillation counter in order to determine whether there was indeed a major contamination problem. Accordingly, I would place roach motels in dark places along the baseboards in every room and hallway in the building. I would leave the roach motels for a few days in order to maximize my capture rate; I would then collect the roach motels, being careful to label each one to indicate where the roaches in it were captured. All roaches and roach by-prod-

233

ucts would be stored behind plexiglass shields, in order to minimize my possible radiation exposure during this experiment. I would then run each captured roach through the scintillation counter (a process which they, alas, would not survive) in order to determine how radioactive they are. As a negative control, I would also capture and count roaches in a place where no radioactive materials are used, such as my graduate student apartment.

Give five points for any protocol (or experimental outline: not every step need be listed in fine detail, but it should be clear what the student intends to test) that is consonant with the hypothesis given in part a (if the two seem to be unrelated, withhold these points); give five points for the presence of a control for the experiment.

d. **(15 points)** A data table showing what data you would collect:

Location	Roach I.D. #	$_{15}P^{32}$ counts per minute

Note: *Accept all reasonable answers, as long as they are consonant with the student's answers to parts a–d.*

Give five points for the presence of a data table; 5 points if there is an independent variable (not necessarily labeled as such) present in the data table headings; and 5 points if there is at least one dependent variable (not necessarily labeled as such) present in the data table headings. In this answer, roach location is the independent variable, and counts per minute is the dependent variable.

e. **(10 points)** A description of how you would use your data to decide whether radioactive roaches did indeed pose a serious contamination problem for the lab building.

In order to be safe, the roaches would have to contain no more $_{15}P^{32}$ than the background level present in the control roaches from my apartment. If they contained significantly more of the isotope than this, and if many roaches from many parts of the building were found to be contaminated, then I would say that the roaches pose a significant contamination problem. I would thus compare the results from the lab roaches with those from the apartment roaches, and see if the lab roaches were indeed significantly more radioactive than the apartment roaches.

Note: *Accept all reasonable answers, as long as they are consonant with the student's answers to parts a–d.*

Give ten points for an answer that explains how the data will be used to come up with a conclusion. If the student doesn't mention the data, then give no points.

Total number of points possible: 50

SCORING PROTOCOL
SYSTEMS ASSESSMENT

A storage facility for spent nuclear reactor fuel can be thought of as a system. For this system, do the following:

1. **(25 points)** List the parts of the system. Include boundaries, elements, input, and output.

   Boundaries: (describe)

   The boundaries of this system are the boundaries of the storage building.

   For ten points total, accept any reasonable <u>closed</u> boundaries, but be sure that the elements, input, and output listed are consistent with them.

   Elements: (list at least five)

   Fuel rods and their parts, including fuel and casing materials; the water in the storage pond, the cement that makes up the pool's walls, the air in the storage building.

   Give one point for each reasonable element up to a maximum of five points.

   Input: (list at least two kinds)

   Air from outside the storage building, insects from outside the storage building, workers and machinery, more depleted fuel rods.

   Give 2.5 points for each listed input item up to a maximum of five points.

   Output: (list at least two kinds)

   Air leaving the storage building, insects leaving the storage building, workers and equipment leaving the storage building; water leaking through cracks in the cement of the pool; fuel rods headed for a more permanent repository.

   Give 2.5 points for each listed output item, up to five points.

2. **(10 points)** Draw a diagram of the system that shows where each of the parts can be found.

   Accept any reasonable diagram.

3. **(15 points total)** On your diagram, draw lines (in a different color) showing three important interactions between different parts of the system. Why is each of these interactions important to the system? Explain your answer.

   a. Interaction #1:

   Water absorbing neutrons produced by the fuel rods: water acts as shielding material.

235

b. Interaction #2:

Radiation and cement walls of storage pool: gradually can reduce the strength of the cement; cement also acts as a shielding material.

c. Interaction #3:

Radiation from decay of fuel interacts with fuel rod casings to reduce their strength.

Accept any reasonable interaction; give five points for each correct answer.

Total number of points possible: 50

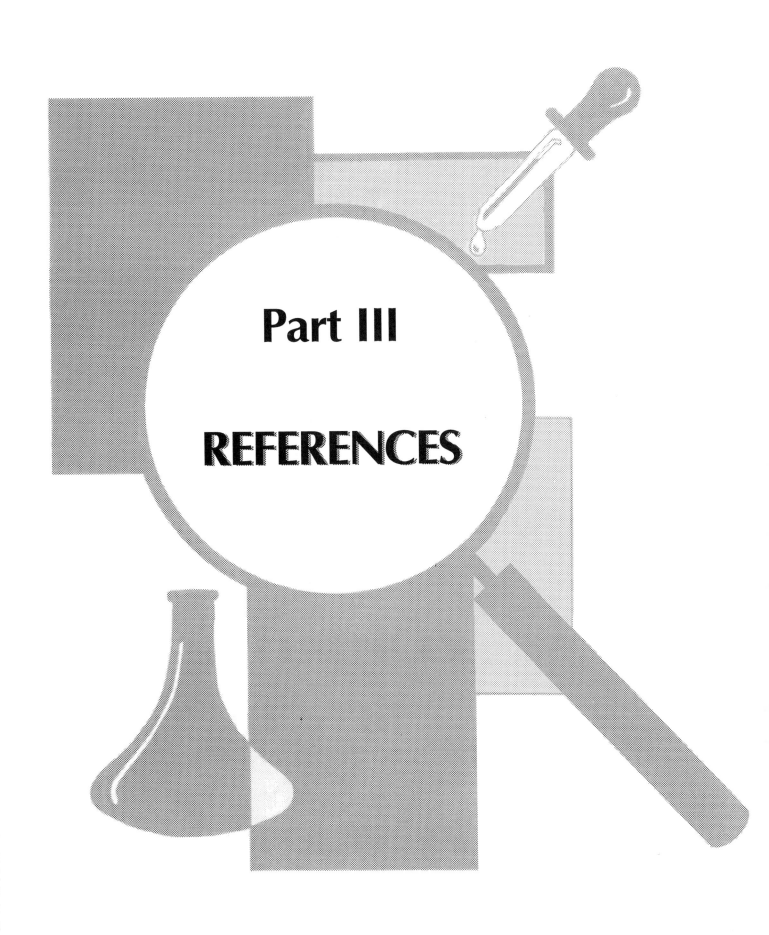

Part III

REFERENCES

REFERENCES

Aftergood, S., Hafemeister, D.W., Prilutsky, O.F., J.R. & Rodionov, S.N. (1991). Nuclear power in space. *Scientific American*, June, 42–47.

Asimov, I. (1965). *New intelligent man's guide to science: The physical sciences.* NY: Basic Books.

Barrows, H.S. (1988). *The tutorial process.* IL: Southern Illinois University School of Medicine.

Byrne, J., Crossett, B., & Bailey, B. (1990). *Tracking down thinking skills: A four-phase model for developing research processes.* National Association for Gifted Children Annual Convention, Little Rock, AR.

Caplan, R. (1990). *Our earth, ourselves.* NY: Bantam Books.

Cothron, J.H., Giese, R.N., & Rezba, R.J. (1996). *Science experiments and projects for students.* Dubuque, IA: Kendall/Hunt Publishing Company.

Cothron, J.H., Giese, R.N., & Rezba, R.J. (1996). *Science experiments by the hundreds.* Dubuque, IA: Kendall/Hunt Publishing Company.

Cothron, J.H., Giese, R.N., & Rezba, R.J. (1996). *Students and research: Practical strategies for science classrooms and competition.* Dubuque, IA: Kendall/Hunt Publishing Company.

Cramer, J., McCarroll, T., & McDowell, H. (1991). Time to choose. *Time*, April 29, 54–61.

Fermi, L. (1954). *Atoms in the family.* Chicago, IL: University of Chicago Press.

Goffman, J.W. (1979). *An irreverent, illustrated view of nuclear power.* CA: Committee for Nuclear Responsibility.

Gould, J.M., & Goldman, B.A. (1991). *Deadly deceit.* NY: Four Walls Eight Windows.

Haber-Schaim, V., Dodge, J.H., & Walter, J.A. (1986). *PSSC physics.* Lexington, MA: D.C. Heath & Company.

Hecht, M.M. (1991). Cold fusion: Good research, bad press. *21st Century Science and Technology*, 16–34.

Kleg, M., & Totten, S. (1990). Horizontal nuclear proliferation: Concepts, issues, and controversies. *Social Education*, March, 133–135.

Kleg, M., & Totten, S. (1990). On teaching horizontal nuclear proliferation: A conceptual framework. *Social Education*, March, 136–142.

Loventhal, P. (1990). The nuclear power and nuclear weapons connection. *Social Education*, March, 146–150.

Levoy, G. (1988). Nukebusters. *Omni*, May, 14.

Martocci, B., & Wilson, G. *A basic guide to nuclear power.* Edison Electric Institute.

Molander, R., & Nichols, R. (1985). *Who will stop the bomb?* NY: Facts on File.

Naar, J. (1990). *Design for a livable planet.* NY: Harper & Row Publishers.

Nair, D. (1987). Chernobyl: Asking the right questions. *The Science Teacher*, November, 25–33.

Nelkin, D. (1987). *Selling science: How the press covers science and technology.* NY: W.H. Freeman & Company.

Parisi, L. (Ed.) (1989). *Hot rods: Storage of spent nuclear fuel.* Boulder, CO: Social Science Education Consortium, Inc.

Pedersen, A. (1991). *Environment book.* Santa Fe, NM: John Muir Publications.

Piasecki, B., & Asmus, P. (1990). *In search of environmental excellence: Moving beyond blame.* NY: Simon & Schuster, Inc.

Project physics (1975). NY: Holt, Rinehart, & Winston, Inc.

Radlauer, E., & Radlauer, R. (1985). *Nuclear tech talk.* Chicago, IL: Children's Press.

Rathjens, G., & Miller, M. (1991). Nuclear proliferation after the cold war. *Technology Review,* August/September, 25–32.

Roberts, L. (1991). The geopolitics of nuclear waste. *Science* 251, February, 864–867.

Weaver, K.F. (1981). Our energy predicament. *National Geographic,* February, 2–23.

Willis, J. (1988). *Earthlets as explained by Professor Xargle.* NY: E.P. Dutton.

Windows on science (1990). Warren, NJ: Optical Data Corporation.

ADDITIONAL REFERENCES UTILIZED WITHIN THE LESSONS

Amateur Scientist column (1952). *Scientific American,* September, 179.

Chernobyl: A chronicle of difficult weeks. Glasnost Film Festival, Vol. #4.

> The Video Project
> 5332 College Avenue, Suite 101
> Oakland, CA 94618
> 1-800-4-PLANET

Consumer Reports , July, 1987 (p. 440), October, 1989 (p. 623), and January, 1990.

Edwards, M. (1994). Living with a monster: Chernobyl. *National Geographic, 186* (2), 100–115.

Meller, P. (1991). Our electric future: A comeback for nuclear power? *National Geographic, 180* (2), 60–89.

OCRUM (1990). *Science, secrecy, and America's nuclear waste: The waste management system.* Washington, DC: U.S. Department of Energy.

> OCRUM Information Center
> Attn: Curriculum Department
> P.O. Box 44375
> Washington, DC 20020
> (800) 225-6972

Our electric future. *National Geographic,* August, 1991, 60–89.

Project Physics. (1975). NY: Holt, Rinehart & Winston, Inc.

Scientific American (1956), December (p. 169), April (p. 156), and June (p. 173).

Shcherbak, Y.M. (1996). Ten years of the Chernobyl era. *Scientific American,* April, 44–49.

Swicord, B. (1984). Debating with gifted fifth and sixth graders. *Gifted Child Quarterly, 28* (3), 127–129.

Windows on Science. (1990). Warren, NJ: Optical Data Corporation.

Whipple, C.G. (1996). Can nuclear waste be stored safely at Yucca Mountain? *Scientific American,* June, 72–79.

Wolfson, R. (1993). *Nuclear choices: A citizen's guide to nuclear technology.* Cambridge, MA: The MIT Press. (ISBN# 0-262-73108-8)

MODULAR UNITS THAT MAY BE INTEGRATED WITH *HOT RODS*

- The Waste Hierarchy
- Investigating Hazardous Materials
- Determining Threshold Limits
    Developed by:
    CEPUP, Lawrence Hall of Science
    Distributed by:
    Innovative Learning Publications (Addison-Wesley)
    Route 128
    Reading, MA 01867
    (800) 552-2259